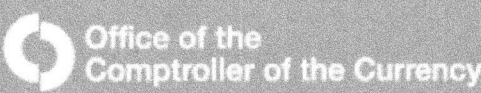

OCC Mortgage Metrics Report

Disclosure of National Bank and Federal Savings
Association Mortgage Loan Data

Fourth Quarter 2013

Office of the Comptroller of the Currency
Washington, D.C.

March 2014

Contents

Executive Summary 4

About Mortgage Metrics 8

Definitions and Method 8

PART I: Mortgage Performance 11

Overall Mortgage Portfolio 11

Overall Mortgage Performance 12

Performance of Mortgages Held by Reporting Banks and Thrift 13

Performance of Government-Guaranteed Mortgages 14

Performance of GSE Mortgages 15

Seriously Delinquent Mortgages, by Risk Category 16

Mortgages 30 to 59 Days Delinquent, by Risk Category 17

PART II: Home Retention Actions 18

A. Loan Modifications, Trial-Period Plans, and Payment Plans 18

New Home Retention Actions 18

HAMP Modifications and Trial-Period Plans, by Investor and Risk Category 19

New Home Retention Actions Relative to Newly Initiated Foreclosures 20

Types of Modification Actions 21

Types of HAMP Modification Actions 22

Types of Modification Actions, by Risk Category 23

Types of Modification Actions, by Investor and Product Type 24

Types of HAMP Modification Actions, by Investor and Product Type 25

Changes in Monthly Payments Resulting From Modification 26

Changes in Monthly Payments Resulting From Modifications, by Quarter 27

Changes in Monthly Payments Resulting From HAMP Modifications, by Quarter 28

Average Change in Monthly Payments Resulting From Modifications, by Quarter 29

B. Modified Loan Performance 30

Re-Default Rates of Modified Loans: 60 or More Days Delinquent 30

Re-Default Rates of Modified Loans: 30 or More Days Delinquent 31

Re-Default Rates of Modified Loans: 90 or More Days Delinquent 32

Re-Default Rate, by Investor (60 or More Days Delinquent)......................................33

Performance of HAMP Modifications Compared With Other Modifications 35

C. Modified Loan Performance, by Change in Monthly Payments.........................36

Re-Default Rates of Loans by Change in Payment 36

60+ Delinquency at Six Months After Modification by Change in Monthly Payment..38

Status of Mortgages Modified in 2008–3Q 2013...39

Part III: Home Forfeiture Actions—Foreclosures, Short Sales, and Deed-in-Lieu-of-Foreclosure Actions 40

Completed Foreclosures and Other Home Forfeiture Actions 40

Newly Initiated Foreclosures..41

Foreclosures in Process 42

Completed Foreclosures...43

Completed Short Sales and Deeds in Lieu of Foreclosure 44

New Home Retention Actions Relative to Forfeiture Actions, by Risk Category........45

Appendixes 46

Appendix A—New Loan Modifications...46

Appendix B—New Trial-Period Plans 47

Appendix C—New Payment Plans 48

Appendix D—Breakdown of Individual and Combination Modification Actions..........49

Appendix E—Mortgage Modification Data by State...51

Index of Tables 61

Index of Figures..64

Executive Summary

This *OCC Mortgage Metrics Report* for the fourth quarter of 2013 provides performance data on first-lien residential mortgages serviced by selected national banks and one federal savings association. The mortgages in this portfolio comprise about 49 percent of all first-lien residential mortgages outstanding in the United States—24.9 million loans totaling $4.2 trillion in unpaid principal. This report provides information on their performance through December 31, 2013.

The performance of mortgages in this portfolio improved for the fifth consecutive quarter. At the end of the fourth quarter of 2013, 91.8 percent of mortgages serviced by the reporting servicers were current and performing, compared with 91.4 percent at the end of the previous quarter and 89.4 percent a year earlier. The percentage of mortgages that were 30 to 59 days past due was 2.6 percent, down 0.8 percent from the previous quarter and 8.7 percent from a year earlier. The percentage of mortgages included in this report that were seriously delinquent—60 or more days past due or held by bankrupt borrowers whose payments were 30 or more days past due—decreased to 3.5 percent of the mortgages in this portfolio compared with 3.6 percent at the end of the previous quarter and 4.4 percent a year earlier. The percentage of mortgages that were seriously delinquent has decreased 20.7 percent from a year earlier.

The number of loans in the process of foreclosure at the end of the fourth quarter of 2013 decreased by 45.9 percent from a year earlier to 523,528. During the quarter, servicers initiated 124,468 new foreclosures—a decrease of 20.6 percent from a year earlier. Factors contributing to the decline include improved economic conditions and aggressive foreclosure prevention assistance, and the transfer of loans to servicers outside the federal banking system. The number of completed foreclosures also decreased to 60,765, a decrease of 26.6 percent from the previous quarter and 42.6 percent from a year earlier.

Servicers implemented 242,828 home retention actions—including modifications, trial-period plans, and shorter-term payment plans—compared with 84,031 home forfeiture actions during the quarter, which include completed foreclosures, short sales, and deed-in-lieu-of-foreclosure actions. The number of home retention actions implemented by servicers decreased by 22.4 percent from the previous quarter and 34.0 percent from a year earlier. Ninety-one percent of modifications in the fourth quarter of 2013 reduced monthly principal and interest payments; 64.6 percent of modifications reduced payments by 20 percent or more. Modifications reduced payments by $344 per month on average, while modifications made under the Home Affordable Modification Program (HAMP) reduced monthly payments by an average of $422.

Mortgage Performance

- The overall percentage of mortgages in this report that were current and performing increased to 91.8 percent at the end of the fourth quarter of 2013 (see table 7).

- The percentage of mortgages that were seriously delinquent at the end of the quarter was 3.5 percent, a decrease of 20.7 percent from a year earlier (see table 7).

- The percentage of government-guaranteed mortgages that were current and performing increased to 86.1 percent from 84.7 percent a year earlier (see table 9). Government-guaranteed mortgages compose 24.6 percent of the total serviced portfolio. The percentage of government-guaranteed mortgages that were seriously delinquent decreased 7.7 percent from a year earlier to 6.5 percent of the government-guaranteed mortgages in the portfolio (see table 9).

- Mortgages serviced for Fannie Mae and Freddie Mac (government-sponsored enterprises or GSE) made up 58.9 percent of the mortgages in this report. The percentage of these mortgages that were current and performing was 95.9 percent at the end of the fourth quarter of 2013, an increase from the previous quarter and from a year earlier (see table 10).

Home Retention Actions: Loan Modifications, Trial-Period Plans, and Payment Plans

- Servicers implemented 242,828 home retention actions—modifications, trial-period plans, and payment plans—during the fourth quarter of 2013 (see table 1). The number of home retention actions was nearly three times the number of completed foreclosures, short sales, and deed-in-lieu-of-foreclosure actions in the quarter (see table 5).

- New home retention actions included 72,466 modifications, 82,269 trial-period plans, and 88,093 payment plans (see table 1). HAMP modifications decreased 10.1 percent from the previous quarter to 20,829. Other modifications decreased to 51,637—a decrease of 32.2 percent from the previous quarter and 54.8 percent from a year earlier. HAMP trial-period plans decreased 19.2 percent from the previous quarter to 31,526, up 24.6 percent from the previous year.

Table 1. Number of New Home Retention Actions							
	12/31/12	3/31/13	6/30/13	9/30/13	12/31/13	1Q %Change	1Y %Change
Other Modifications	114,181	110,519	85,582	76,134	51,637	-32.2%	-54.8%
HAMP Modifications	29,314	28,030	22,613	23,159	20,829	-10.1%	-28.9%
Other Trial-Period Plans	96,424	85,516	68,465	62,163	50,743	-18.4%	-47.4%
HAMP Trial-Period Plans	25,306	18,145	32,028	38,999	31,526	-19.2%	24.6%
Payment Plans	102,446	107,113	107,403	112,568	88,093	-21.7%	-14.0%
Total	367,671	349,323	316,091	313,023	242,828	-22.4%	-34.0%

- Servicers reduced interest rates in 76.7 percent of all modifications made during the fourth quarter of 2013. Servicers used term extensions in 75.9 percent of modifications, principal deferrals in 30.6 percent, and principal reductions in 10.5 percent (see table 17). Among HAMP modifications, servicers reduced interest rates in 90.3 percent of those modifications, deferred principal in 26.3 percent, and reduced principal in 15.6 percent (see table 18).

- Servicers have reduced monthly principal and interest payments in 91.0 percent of modifications made in the quarter (see table 22). Servicers reduced monthly payments by an average of 26.6 percent for all borrowers who qualified for modifications. HAMP modifications reduced payments by an average of 31.5 percent (see table 24).

Modified Loan Performance

- Servicers modified 3,388,010 mortgages from the beginning of 2008 through the end of the third quarter of 2013. At the end of the fourth quarter of 2013, 43.4 percent of these modifications were current or paid off. Another 5.9 percent were 30 to 59 days delinquent, and 10.7 percent were seriously delinquent. Another 4.3 percent were in the process of foreclosure, and 8.0 percent had completed the foreclosure process (see table 2).

Table 2. Status of Mortgages Modified in 2008–3Q 2013								
	Total	Current	30–59 Days Delinquent	Seriously Delinquent	Foreclosures in Process	Completed Foreclosures	Paid Off	No Longer in the Portfolio*
2008	443,294	19.0%	3.8%	8.2%	4.0%	17.0%	4.7%	43.2%
2009	593,884	28.4%	4.8%	10.5%	4.8%	13.2%	4.5%	33.8%
2010	955,422	37.6%	5.5%	10.5%	4.8%	8.8%	3.5%	29.3%
2011	569,553	44.7%	6.2%	11.8%	4.9%	4.5%	2.7%	25.2%
2012	479,820	56.7%	7.3%	12.3%	4.2%	1.2%	1.6%	16.7%
2013	346,037	65.6%	8.9%	11.0%	2.1%	0.2%	0.6%	11.5%
Total	3,388,010	40.3%	5.9%	10.7%	4.3%	8.0%	3.1%	27.6%
HAMP Modification Performance Compared With Other Modifications**								
Other Modifications	1,845,827	43.9%	7.0%	13.3%	5.0%	6.6%	3.1%	21.1%
HAMP Modifications	761,043	51.0%	4.9%	6.5%	2.9%	3.6%	1.9%	29.2%
Modifications That Reduced Payments by 10 Percent or More								
	2,163,438	46.1%	5.9%	9.3%	3.6%	5.4%	2.3%	27.3%
Modifications That Reduced Payments by Less Than 10 Percent								
	1,224,572	30.0%	5.8%	13.3%	5.6%	12.5%	4.6%	28.2%

*Processing constraints prevented some servicers from reporting the reason for removal from the portfolio.

**Modifications used to compare with HAMP modifications include only modifications implemented from the third quarter of 2009 through the third quarter of 2013.

- HAMP modifications have performed better than other modifications. Of the 761,043 HAMP modifications implemented since the third quarter of 2009, 52.9 percent were current or paid off at the end of the fourth quarter of 2013, compared with 47.0 percent of other modifications (see table 2). HAMP modifications perform better because of the emphasis on reduced monthly payments, affordability relative to income, income verification, and successful completion of a trial period. While HAMP modifications generally reduce the borrowers' monthly payments more and perform better over time, more restrictive criteria limit the number of borrowers who may qualify for a HAMP modification.

- At the end of the fourth quarter of 2013, 48.4 percent of modifications that reduced payments by 10 percent or more were current or paid off, compared with 34.6 percent of those that reduced payments by less than 10 percent (see table 2).

- Modifications on mortgages owned by the servicers and those serviced for the GSEs performed better than other modifications. Of the modifications implemented from January 1, 2008, 20.2 percent of modifications on mortgages held in the servicers' own portfolios, 23.6 percent of Fannie Mae mortgages, and 22.7 percent of Freddie Mac mortgages were 60 or more days delinquent after 12 months. Conversely, 44.6 percent of government-guaranteed mortgages and 39.1 percent of private investor-held loans were 60 or more days delinquent after 12 months. This variance reflects differences in the loans, the modification programs, and the servicers' flexibility to modify loans they own (see table 3).

Table 3. Re-Default Rates for Portfolio Loans and Loans Serviced for Others (60 or More Days Delinquent)*					
Investor Loan Type	6 Months After Modification	12 Months After Modification	18 Months After Modification	24 Months After Modification	36 Months After Modification
Fannie Mae	16.4%	23.6%	27.0%	27.9%	27.9%
Freddie Mac	15.9%	22.7%	26.6%	27.9%	28.5%
Government-Guaranteed	29.9%	44.6%	50.6%	52.1%	54.0%
Private	29.3%	39.1%	44.6%	46.4%	49.5%
Portfolio Loans	12.7%	20.2%	24.9%	26.4%	28.0%
Overall	22.0%	31.4%	36.3%	37.9%	39.7%

*Data include all modifications made since January 1, 2008, that have aged the indicated number of months.

Foreclosures and Other Home Forfeiture Actions

- Newly initiated foreclosures decreased 4.7 percent from the previous quarter and 20.6 percent from a year earlier. The number of foreclosures in process decreased 13.4 percent from the previous quarter and 45.9 percent from a year earlier (see table 4). Factors contributing to the decline include improved economic conditions, foreclosure prevention assistance, the completion of foreclosures, and transfer of loans to servicers outside the federal banking system.

Table 4. New Foreclosures and Foreclosures in Process							
	12/31/12	3/31/13	6/30/13	9/30/13	12/31/13	1Q %Change	1Y %Change
Newly Initiated Foreclosures	156,773	178,360	150,592	130,592	124,468	-4.7%	-20.6%
Foreclosures in Process	967,467	907,228	744,369	604,763	523,528	-13.4%	-45.9%

- Home forfeiture actions totaled 84,031 at the end of the quarter, a decrease of 27.7 percent from the previous quarter and 50.3 percent from a year earlier. Completed foreclosures decreased 26.6 percent from the previous quarter and 42.6 percent from a year earlier. Short sales decreased 32.3 percent from the previous quarter and 65.8 percent from a year earlier. Short sales composed 25.2 percent of home forfeiture actions (see table 5).

Table 5. Completed Foreclosures and Other Home Forfeiture Actions							
	12/31/12	3/31/13	6/30/13	9/30/13	12/31/13	1Q %Change	1Y %Change
Completed Foreclosures	105,875	84,977	79,960	82,841	60,765	-26.6%	-42.6%
New Short Sales	61,761	43,143	39,207	31,261	21,149	-32.3%	-65.8%
New Deed-in-Lieu-of-Foreclosure Actions	1,428	3,596	2,579	2,112	2,117	0.2%	48.2%
Total	169,064	131,716	121,746	116,214	84,031	-27.7%	-50.3%

About Mortgage Metrics

The *OCC Mortgage Metrics Report* presents data on first-lien residential mortgages serviced by seven national banks and a federal savings association with the largest mortgage-servicing portfolios.[1] The data represent 49 percent of all first-lien residential mortgages outstanding in the country and focus on credit performance, loss mitigation efforts, and foreclosures. More than 91 percent of the mortgages in the portfolio were serviced for investors other than the reporting institutions. At the end of the fourth quarter of 2013, the reporting institutions serviced 24.9 million first-lien mortgage loans, totaling $4.2 trillion in unpaid principal (see table 6).

The loans reflected in this report represent a large percentage of the overall mortgage industry, but they do not represent a statistically random sample of all mortgage loans. The characteristics of these loans may differ from the overall population of mortgages. This report does not attempt to quantify or adjust for known seasonal effects that occur within the mortgage industry.

In addition to providing information to the public, the report and its data support the supervision of national bank and federal savings association mortgage-servicing practices. Examiners use the data to help assess emerging trends, identify anomalies, compare servicers with peers, evaluate asset quality and necessary loan-loss reserves, and assess loss mitigation actions.

The report promotes the use of standardized terms and elements, which allow better comparisons across the industry and over time. The report uses standardized definitions for prime, Alt-A, and subprime mortgages based on commonly used credit score ranges.

The Office of the Comptroller of the Currency (OCC) and the participating institutions devote significant resources to ensuring that the information is reliable and accurate. Steps to ensure the validity of the data include quality assurance processes conducted by the banks and savings association, comprehensive data validation tests performed by a third-party data aggregator, and comparisons with the institutions' quarterly call reports. Data sets of this size and scope inevitably incur some degree of imperfections. The OCC requires servicers to adjust previous data submissions when errors and omissions are detected. In some cases, data presented in this report reflect resubmissions from institutions that restate and correct earlier information.

The report also includes mortgage modification data by state and territories in appendix E. These data fulfill reporting requirements in the Dodd–Frank Wall Street Reform and Consumer Protection Act of 2010 (Public Law 111-203).

Definitions and Method

The report uses standard definitions for three categories of mortgage creditworthiness based on the following ranges of borrowers' credit scores at the time of origination:

---

[1] The seven national banks are Bank of America, JPMorgan Chase, Citibank, HSBC, PNC, U.S. Bank, and Wells Fargo. The federal savings association is OneWest Bank.

- **Prime**—660 and above.

- **Alt-A**—620 to 659.

- **Subprime**—below 620.

Approximately 9 percent of mortgages in the portfolio were not accompanied by credit scores and are classified as "other." This group includes a mix of prime, Alt-A, and subprime mortgages. The lack of credit scores often results from acquisitions of portfolios from third parties for which borrower credit scores at origination were not available.

Additional definitions include:

- **Completed foreclosures**—Ownership of properties transferred to servicers or investors. The ultimate result is the loss of borrowers' homes because of nonpayment.

- **Deed-in-lieu-of-foreclosure actions**—Actions in which borrowers transfer ownership of the properties (deeds) to servicers in full satisfaction of the outstanding mortgage debt to lessen the adverse impact of the debt on borrowers' credit records. Deed-in-lieu-of-foreclosure actions typically have a less adverse impact than foreclosures on borrowers' credit records.

- **Foreclosures in process**—Number of mortgages for which servicers have begun formal foreclosure proceedings but have not yet completed the foreclosure process. The foreclosure process varies by state and can take 15 months or more to complete. Many foreclosures in process never result in the loss of borrowers' homes because servicers simultaneously pursue other loss mitigation actions, and borrowers may return their mortgages to current and performing status.

- **Government-guaranteed mortgages**—All mortgages with an explicit guaranty from the U.S. government, including the Federal Housing Administration (FHA), the Department of Veterans Affairs (VA), and, to a lesser extent, certain other departments. These loans may be held in pools backing Government National Mortgage Association (Ginnie Mae) securities, owned by or securitized through different third-party investors, or held in the portfolios of reporting institutions.

- **Home retention actions**—Loan modifications, trial-period plans, and payment plans that allow borrowers to retain ownership and occupancy of their homes while attempting to return the loans to a current and performing status.

- **Loan modifications**—Actions that contractually change the terms of mortgages with respect to interest rates, maturity, principal, or other terms of the loan.

- **Newly initiated foreclosures**—Mortgages for which the servicers initiate formal foreclosure proceedings during the quarter. Many newly initiated foreclosures do not result in the loss of borrowers' homes because servicers simultaneously pursue other loss mitigation actions, and borrowers may act to return their mortgages to current and performing status.

- **Payment plans**—Short-to-medium-term changes in scheduled terms and payments in order to return mortgages to a current and performing status.

- **Payment-option, adjustable rate mortgages (ARM)**—Mortgages that allow borrowers to choose a monthly payment that may initially reduce principal, pay interest only, or result in negative amortization, when some amount of unpaid interest is added to the unpaid principal of the loan and results in an increased balance.

- **Principal deferral modifications**—Modifications that remove a portion of the unpaid principal from the amount used to calculate monthly principal and interest payments for a set period. The deferred amount becomes due at the end of the loan term.

- **Principal reduction modifications**—Modifications that permanently forgive a portion of the unpaid principal owed on a mortgage.

- **Re-default rates**—Percentage of modified loans that subsequently become delinquent or enter the foreclosure process. As measures of delinquency, this report presents re-default rates using 30, 60, and 90 or more days delinquent and in process of foreclosure. It focuses on the 60-day-delinquent measure. All re-default data presented in this report are based on modified loans in effect for the specified amount of time after the modification. All loans that have been repaid in full, been refinanced, been sold, or completed the foreclosure process are removed from the calculation. Data include only modifications that have had time to age the indicated number of months following the modification.

- **Seriously delinquent loans**—Mortgages that are 60 or more days past due, and all mortgages held by bankrupt borrowers whose payments are 30 or more days past due.

- **Short sales**—Sales of the mortgaged properties at prices that net less than the total amount due on the mortgages. Servicers and borrowers negotiate repayment programs, forbearance, or forgiveness for any remaining deficiency on the debt. Short sales typically have a less adverse impact than foreclosures on borrowers' credit records.

- **Trial-period plans**—Home retention actions that allow borrowers to demonstrate capability and willingness to pay their modified mortgages for a set period of time. The action becomes permanent following the successful completion of the trial period.

Loan delinquencies are reported using the Mortgage Bankers Association convention that a loan is past due when a scheduled payment has not been made by the due date of the following scheduled payment. The statistics and calculated ratios are based on the number of loans rather than on the dollar amount outstanding.

Percentages are rounded to one decimal place unless the result is less than 0.1 percent, which is rounded to two decimal places. The report uses whole numbers when approximating. Values in tables may not total 100 percent because of rounding.

In tables throughout this report, the quarters are indicated by the last day of the quarter (e.g., 12/31/13), quarter-to-quarter changes are shown under the "1Q %Change" column, and year-to-year changes are shown under the "1Y %Change" column.

In tables throughout this report, percentages shown under "1Q %Change" and "1Y %Change" are calculated using actual data, not the rounded values reported for each quarter. Calculating period-to-period changes from the rounded values reported in the tables may yield materially different values than those values indicated in the table.

Mortgage Metrics Report data may not agree with other published data because of timing differences in updating servicer-processing systems.

PART I: Mortgage Performance

Part I describes the performance of the overall mortgage portfolio, mortgages owned and held by the reporting banks and savings association, government-guaranteed mortgages, mortgages serviced for the GSEs, and mortgages within each risk category.

Overall Mortgage Portfolio

At the end of the fourth quarter of 2013, the portfolio of mortgages in this report included 24.9 million loans with $4.2 trillion in unpaid principal. The number of mortgages in the portfolio decreased 14.1 percent from a year earlier. The unpaid principal of those loans decreased 14.4 percent from a year earlier. Prime loans were 75.0 percent of the servicing portfolio at the end of the quarter. Subprime loans were 6.0 percent of the servicing portfolio at the end of the quarter, while Alt-A loans were 10.0 percent. The percentage of prime loans has increased because of a higher number of defaults of lower quality loans, increased origination of prime loans, and some loans being sold to nonreporting servicers.

Table 6. Overall Mortgage Portfolio					
	12/31/12	3/31/13	6/30/13	9/30/13	12/31/13
Total Servicing (Millions)	$4,910,150	$4,740,528	$4,507,984	$4,357,767	$4,205,140
Total Servicing (Number of Loans)	28,979,134	27,941,336	26,528,415	25,643,169	24,902,063
Composition (Percentage of All Mortgages in the Portfolio)					
Prime	72%	73%	73%	74%	75%
Alt-A	11%	11%	10%	10%	10%
Subprime	7%	7%	7%	6%	6%
Other	10%	10%	10%	9%	9%
Composition (Number of Loans in Each Risk Category of the Portfolio)					
Prime	20,990,451	20,284,238	19,451,032	18,973,544	18,598,018
Alt-A	3,114,517	2,993,971	2,781,584	2,631,270	2,529,860
Subprime	1,991,912	1,908,482	1,749,154	1,630,463	1,522,461
Other	2,882,254	2,754,645	2,546,645	2,407,892	2,251,724

Figure 1. Portfolio Composition
Percentage of All Mortgage Loans in the Portfolio

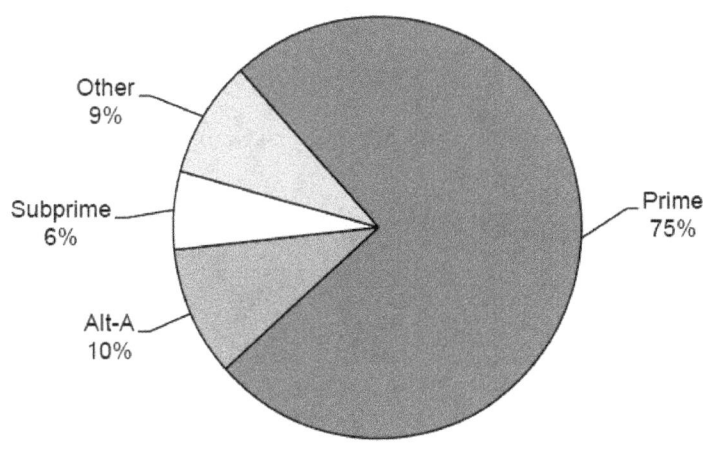

Overall Mortgage Performance

The performance of mortgages included in this report has improved for five consecutive quarters. The percentage of mortgages that were current and performing at the end of the quarter was 91.8 percent, compared with 91.4 percent in the previous quarter and 89.4 percent a year earlier. The percentage of mortgages that were 30 to 59 days past due was 2.6 percent, a decrease of 0.8 percent from the previous quarter and 8.7 percent from a year earlier. The percentage of mortgages that were seriously delinquent was 3.5 percent, a decrease of 3.5 percent from the previous quarter and 20.7 percent from a year earlier. The percentage of mortgages in the foreclosure process at the end of the quarter was 2.1 percent, a decrease of 10.9 percent from the previous quarter and 37.0 percent from a year earlier. The number of mortgages in the foreclosure process at the end of the quarter was down 45.9 percent from a year earlier.

Table 7. Overall Portfolio Performance							
(Percentage of Mortgages in the Portfolio)							
	12/31/12	3/31/13	6/30/13	9/30/13	12/31/13	1Q %Change	1Y %Change
Current and Performing	89.4%	90.2%	90.6%	91.4%	91.8%	0.4%	2.7%
30–59 Days Delinquent	2.9%	2.6%	2.9%	2.6%	2.6%	-0.8%	-8.7%
The Following Three Categories Are Classified as Seriously Delinquent							
60–89 Days Delinquent	1.1%	0.9%	0.9%	0.9%	1.0%	1.9%	-10.8%
90 or More Days Delinquent	2.3%	2.1%	1.9%	1.8%	1.7%	-4.1%	-25.5%
Bankruptcy 30 or More Days Delinquent	1.0%	1.0%	1.0%	0.9%	0.8%	-7.9%	-20.2%
Subtotal for Seriously Delinquent	**4.4%**	**4.0%**	**3.8%**	**3.6%**	**3.5%**	**-3.5%**	**-20.7%**
Foreclosures in Process	3.3%	3.2%	2.8%	2.4%	2.1%	-10.9%	-37.0%
(Number of Mortgages in the Portfolio)							
Current and Performing	25,907,686	25,198,157	24,024,452	23,435,693	22,859,232	-2.5%	-11.8%
30–59 Days Delinquent	826,415	717,532	760,078	673,117	648,294	-3.7%	-21.6%
The Following Three Categories Are Classified as Seriously Delinquent							
60–89 Days Delinquent	309,776	248,454	243,832	239,904	237,412	-1.0%	-23.4%
90 or More Days Delinquent	664,007	591,879	499,148	456,887	425,347	-6.9%	-35.9%
Bankruptcy 30 or More Days Delinquent	303,783	278,086	256,536	232,805	208,250	-10.5%	-31.4%
Subtotal for Seriously Delinquent	**1,277,566**	**1,118,419**	**999,516**	**929,596**	**871,009**	**-6.3%**	**-31.8%**
Foreclosures in Process	967,467	907,228	744,369	604,763	523,528	-13.4%	-45.9%
Total	28,979,134	27,941,336	26,528,415	25,643,169	24,902,063	-2.9%	-14.1%

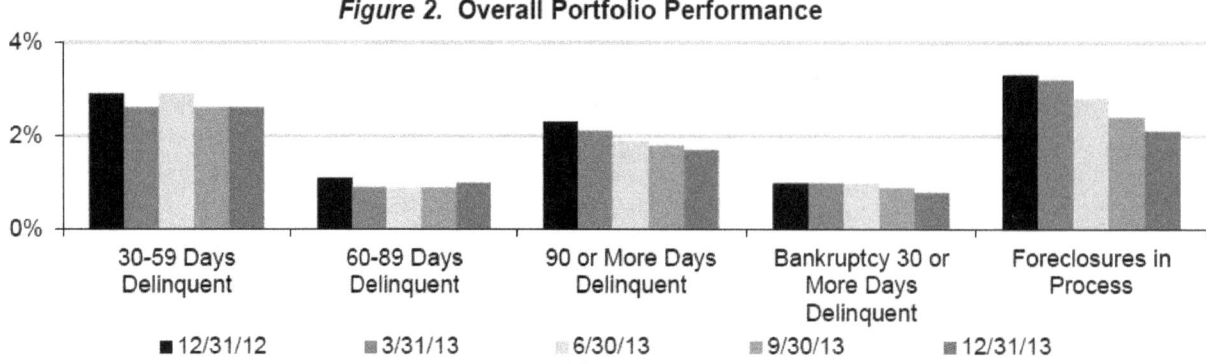

Figure 2. Overall Portfolio Performance

Performance of Mortgages Held by Reporting Banks and Thrift

The eight reporting institutions owned 8.9 percent of the mortgages in this report at the end of 2013, an increase in share from 8.3 percent a year earlier. The percentage of these mortgages that were current at the end of 2013 was 87.4 percent. The percentage of these mortgages that were 30 to 59 days delinquent was 3.3 percent, a decrease of 1.9 percent from a year earlier. The percentage of these mortgages that were seriously delinquent was 5.4 percent, a decrease of 5.6 percent from a year earlier. The percentage of these mortgages in the process of foreclosure was 3.9 percent, a decrease of 21.7 percent from a year earlier. Since 2009, mortgages owned by the servicers have performed worse than mortgages serviced for GSEs because of concentrations in nontraditional loans, weaker markets and delinquent loans repurchased from investors.

Table 8. Performance of Mortgages Held by Reporting Banks and Thrift (Percentage)*						1Q %Change	1Y %Change
	12/31/12	3/31/13	6/30/13	9/30/13	12/31/13		
Current and Performing	85.9%	86.6%	86.6%	87.1%	87.4%	0.4%	1.7%
30–59 Days Delinquent	3.3%	3.1%	3.4%	3.3%	3.3%	0.3%	-1.9%
The Following Three Categories Are Classified as Seriously Delinquent							
60–89 Days Delinquent	1.4%	1.2%	1.3%	1.3%	1.4%	4.3%	2.0%
90 or More Days Delinquent	2.9%	2.7%	2.6%	2.6%	2.5%	-4.0%	-14.5%
Bankruptcy 30 or More Days Delinquent	1.4%	1.5%	1.6%	1.6%	1.5%	-2.3%	4.9%
Subtotal for Seriously Delinquent	5.7%	5.5%	5.5%	5.5%	5.4%	-1.5%	-5.6%
Foreclosures in Process	5.0%	4.8%	4.5%	4.2%	3.9%	-6.1%	-21.7%
Performance of Mortgages Held by Reporting Banks and Thrift (Number)							
Current and Performing	2,071,640	2,133,762	2,059,325	1,997,134	1,943,856	-2.7%	-6.2%
30–59 Days Delinquent	80,196	77,577	80,314	74,648	72,595	-2.8%	-9.5%
The Following Three Categories Are Classified as Seriously Delinquent							
60–89 Days Delinquent	33,072	30,218	30,784	30,782	31,121	1.1%	-5.9%
90 or More Days Delinquent	70,030	67,270	62,544	59,376	55,269	-6.9%	-21.1%
Bankruptcy 30 or More Days Delinquent	34,854	37,976	36,970	35,591	33,736	-5.2%	-3.2%
Subtotal for Seriously Delinquent	137,956	135,464	130,298	125,749	120,126	-4.5%	-12.9%
Foreclosures in Process	120,600	118,292	107,493	95,643	87,120	-8.9%	-27.8%
Total	2,410,392	2,465,095	2,377,430	2,293,174	2,223,697	-3.0%	-7.7%

*The data in this table exclude government-guaranteed mortgages owned and held by the reporting institutions.

Figure 3. Performance of Mortgages Held by Reporting Banks and Thrift

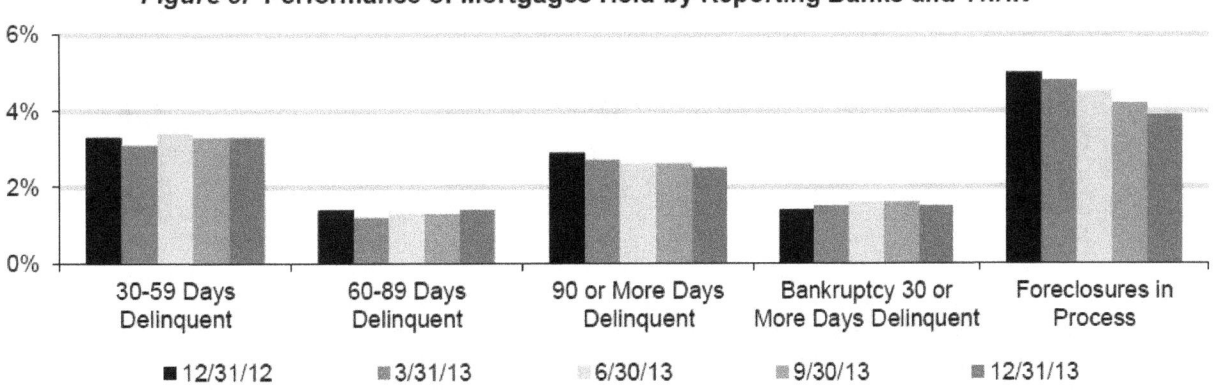

Performance of Government-Guaranteed Mortgages

Government-guaranteed mortgages were 24.6 percent of the loans in this report at the end of the fourth quarter of 2013, an increase in share from 23.7 percent a year ago. The percentage of these mortgages that were current at the end of the quarter was 86.1 percent, up from 84.7 percent a year earlier. The percentage of loans that were 30 to 59 days delinquent was 4.6 percent at the end of 2013, an increase of 1.5 percent from the previous quarter but a decrease of 2.3 percent from a year earlier. The percentage of these loans that were seriously delinquent was 6.5 percent at the end of 2013, an increase of 3.5 percent from the previous quarter but a decrease of 7.7 percent from a year earlier. The percentage of these loans in the process of foreclosure was 2.8 percent, a decrease of 20.6 percent from a year earlier.

Table 9. Performance of Government-Guaranteed Mortgages (Percentage)							
	12/31/12	3/31/13	6/30/13	9/30/13	12/31/13	1Q %Change	1Y %Change
Current and Performing	84.7%	86.2%	85.7%	86.2%	86.1%	-0.2%	1.6%
30–59 Days Delinquent	4.7%	4.1%	4.8%	4.5%	4.6%	1.5%	-2.3%
The Following Three Categories Are Classified as Seriously Delinquent							
60–89 Days Delinquent	1.8%	1.4%	1.6%	1.7%	1.8%	5.3%	-1.4%
90 or More Days Delinquent	4.0%	3.6%	3.4%	3.4%	3.6%	4.5%	-12.0%
Bankruptcy 30 or More Days Delinquent	1.2%	1.2%	1.2%	1.2%	1.2%	-1.8%	-2.7%
Subtotal for Seriously Delinquent	7.1%	6.2%	6.2%	6.3%	6.5%	3.5%	-7.7%
Foreclosures in Process	3.5%	3.6%	3.3%	2.9%	2.8%	-4.4%	-20.6%
Performance of Government-Guaranteed Mortgages (Number)							
Current and Performing	5,820,605	5,897,284	5,592,058	5,398,697	5,274,464	-2.3%	-9.4%
30–59 Days Delinquent	324,524	277,426	313,250	284,697	282,698	-0.7%	-12.9%
The Following Three Categories Are Classified as Seriously Delinquent							
60–89 Days Delinquent	124,342	95,947	102,475	105,993	109,272	3.1%	-12.1%
90 or More Days Delinquent	277,684	246,953	222,428	213,035	217,842	2.3%	-21.6%
Bankruptcy 30 or More Days Delinquent	85,500	80,962	81,430	77,129	74,144	-3.9%	-13.3%
Subtotal for Seriously Delinquent	487,526	423,862	406,333	396,157	401,258	1.3%	-17.7%
Foreclosures in Process	240,345	243,132	216,324	181,965	170,180	-6.5%	-29.2%
Total	6,873,000	6,841,704	6,527,965	6,261,516	6,128,600	-2.1%	-10.8%

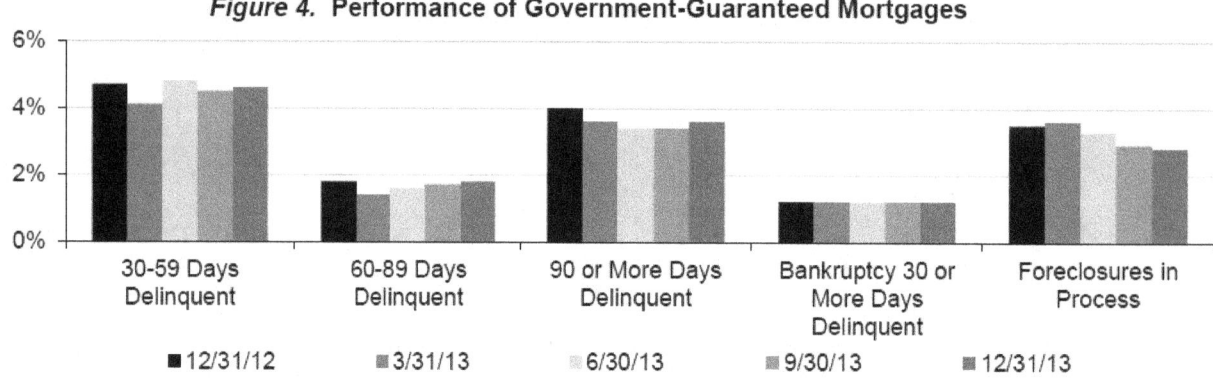

Figure 4. Performance of Government-Guaranteed Mortgages

Performance of GSE Mortgages

GSE mortgages made up 58.9 percent of the mortgages in this report, an increase in share from 57.9 percent a year earlier. GSE mortgages perform better than the overall portfolio because they contain more prime loans. The percentage of GSE mortgages that were current at the end of the quarter was 95.9 percent, up from 94.0 percent a year earlier. The percentage of GSE mortgages that were 30 to 59 days delinquent was 1.4 percent, a decrease of 17.9 percent from a year earlier. The percentage of GSE mortgages that were seriously delinquent was 1.5 percent at the end of the quarter, a decrease of 31.9 percent from a year earlier. The percentage of these loans in the foreclosure process was 1.2 percent, a decrease of 42.5 percent from a year earlier. Fifty-seven percent of the GSE mortgages were serviced for Fannie Mae and 43 percent for Freddie Mac.

Table 10. Performance of GSE Mortgages (Percentage)							
	12/31/12	3/31/13	6/30/13	9/30/13	12/31/13	1Q %Change	1Y %Change
Current and Performing	94.0%	94.6%	95.1%	95.7%	95.9%	0.2%	2.0%
30–59 Days Delinquent	1.8%	1.5%	1.6%	1.4%	1.4%	0.9%	-17.9%
The Following Three Categories Are Classified as Seriously Delinquent							
60–89 Days Delinquent	0.6%	0.5%	0.4%	0.4%	0.5%	4.0%	-21.1%
90 or More Days Delinquent	1.0%	0.9%	0.8%	0.7%	0.6%	-6.4%	-36.9%
Bankruptcy 30 or More Days Delinquent	0.6%	0.5%	0.5%	0.4%	0.4%	-7.2%	-33.7%
Subtotal for Seriously Delinquent	2.2%	1.9%	1.7%	1.5%	1.5%	-3.7%	-31.9%
Foreclosures in Process	2.0%	1.9%	1.5%	1.3%	1.2%	-8.9%	-42.5%
Performance of GSE Mortgages (Number)							
Current and Performing	15,780,823	14,970,222	14,415,761	14,202,109	14,068,620	-0.9%	-10.8%
30–59 Days Delinquent	295,214	244,073	248,747	212,335	211,814	-0.2%	-28.3%
The Following Three Categories Are Classified as Seriously Delinquent							
60–89 Days Delinquent	97,293	74,386	67,829	65,255	67,106	2.8%	-31.0%
90 or More Days Delinquent	169,939	145,282	113,809	101,216	93,692	-7.4%	-44.9%
Bankruptcy 30 or More Days Delinquent	100,114	83,583	70,996	63,155	57,990	-8.2%	-42.1%
Subtotal for Seriously Delinquent	367,346	303,251	252,634	229,626	218,788	-4.7%	-40.4%
Foreclosures in Process	339,817	302,270	233,967	189,610	170,779	-9.9%	-49.7%
Total	16,783,200	15,819,816	15,151,109	14,833,680	14,670,001	-1.1%	-12.6%

Figure 5. Performance of GSE Mortgages

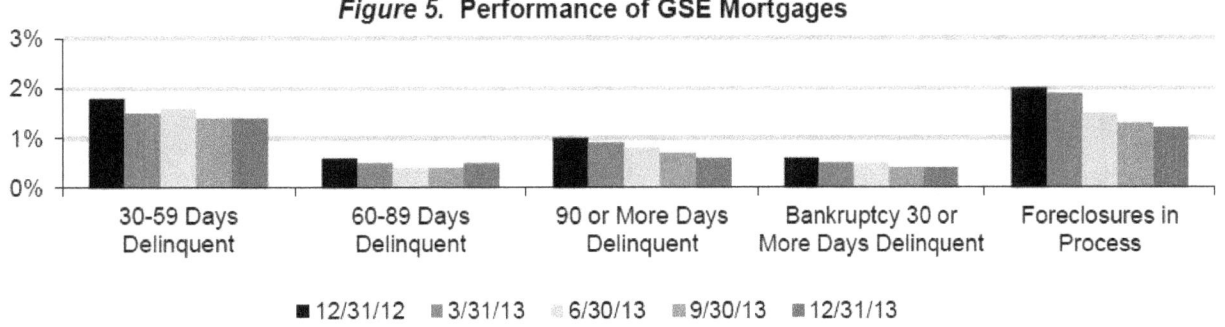

Seriously Delinquent Mortgages, by Risk Category

The portfolio contained 406,557 fewer seriously delinquent loans at the end of the fourth quarter of 2013 than a year earlier—a 31.8 percent decrease. Seriously delinquent loans were 3.5 percent of the portfolio at the end of the quarter, a decrease of 20.7 percent from a year earlier and the lowest level in the six years since the inception of this report. The number of seriously delinquent loans decreased from both the previous quarter and the previous year across all risk categories.

Table 11. Seriously Delinquent Mortgages, by Risk Category							
(Percentage of Mortgages in Each Category)							
	12/31/12	3/31/13	6/30/13	9/30/13	12/31/13	1Q %Change	1Y %Change
Prime	2.3%	2.1%	1.9%	1.8%	1.6%	-7.0%	-29.6%
Alt-A	9.3%	8.4%	8.3%	8.3%	8.4%	0.9%	-10.0%
Subprime	16.0%	14.6%	14.5%	14.6%	14.7%	0.8%	-7.9%
Other	6.2%	5.6%	5.6%	5.7%	5.7%	0.5%	-7.6%
Overall	4.4%	4.0%	3.8%	3.6%	3.5%	-3.5%	-20.7%
(Number of Mortgages in Each Category)							
Prime	490,427	431,353	372,519	335,590	305,796	-8.9%	-37.6%
Alt-A	290,262	252,990	231,168	218,764	212,203	-3.0%	-26.9%
Subprime	318,823	278,647	254,085	238,446	224,412	-5.9%	-29.6%
Other	178,054	155,429	141,744	136,796	128,598	-6.0%	-27.8%
Total	1,277,566	1,118,419	999,516	929,596	871,009	-6.3%	-31.8%

Figure 6. Seriously Delinquent Mortgages, by Risk Category
Percentage of Mortgages in Each Category

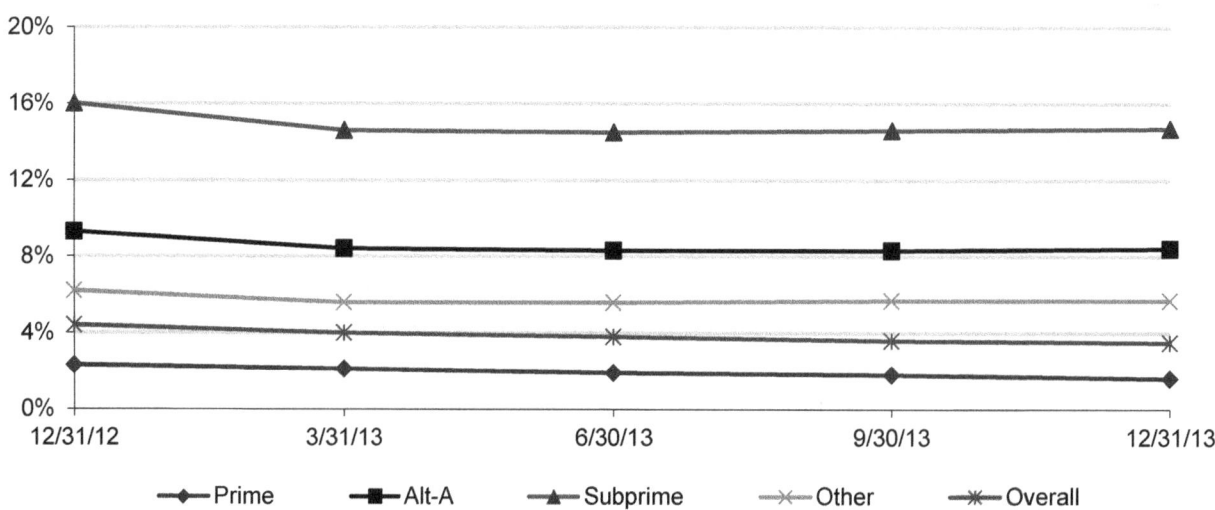

Mortgages 30 to 59 Days Delinquent, by Risk Category

The percentage of loans that were 30 to 59 days delinquent was 2.6 percent of the portfolio at the end of the fourth quarter of 2013, a decrease of 8.7 percent from a year earlier and the lowest year-end level since reporting began in January 2008.

	12/31/12	3/31/13	6/30/13	9/30/13	12/31/13	1Q %Change	1Y %Change
Table 12. **Mortgages 30 to 59 Days Delinquent, by Risk Category** (Percentage of Mortgages in Each Category)							
Prime	1.5%	1.3%	1.4%	1.3%	1.3%	-1.1%	-13.7%
Alt-A	6.4%	5.7%	6.6%	6.2%	6.4%	2.0%	-0.5%
Subprime	9.4%	8.6%	10.0%	9.5%	9.6%	1.0%	1.6%
Other	4.5%	4.2%	4.8%	4.6%	4.6%	1.6%	3.3%
Overall	2.9%	2.6%	2.9%	2.6%	2.6%	-0.8%	-8.7%
(Number of Mortgages in Each Category)							
Prime	309,818	267,211	279,111	244,277	236,900	-3.0%	-23.5%
Alt-A	199,294	170,084	184,916	164,185	161,013	-1.9%	-19.2%
Subprime	188,071	164,998	174,660	154,832	146,067	-5.7%	-22.3%
Other	129,232	115,239	121,391	109,823	104,314	-5.0%	-19.3%
Total	826,415	717,532	760,078	673,117	648,294	-3.7%	-21.6%

Figure 7. **Mortgages 30 to 59 Days Delinquent, by Risk Category**
Percentage of Mortgages in Each Category

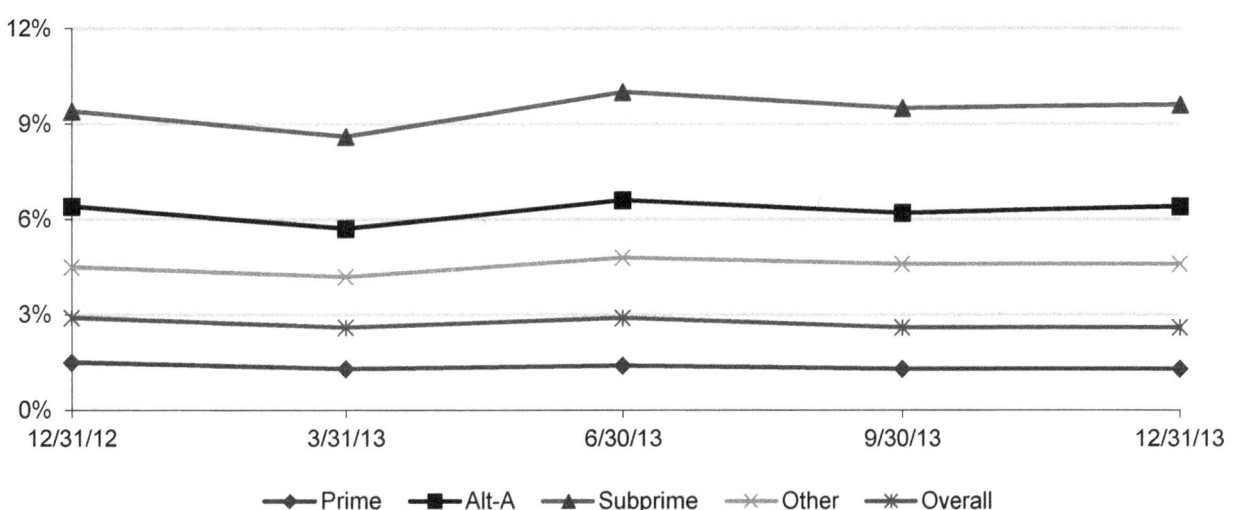

PART II: Home Retention Actions

Home retention actions include loan modifications, in which servicers modify one or more mortgage contract terms; trial-period plans, in which the loans will be converted to modifications upon successful completion of the trial periods; and payment plans, in which no terms are contractually modified but borrowers are given time to catch up on missed payments. All of these actions can help the borrower become current on the loan, attain payment sustainability, and retain the home.

A. Loan Modifications, Trial-Period Plans, and Payment Plans

New Home Retention Actions

Servicers implemented 242,828 home retention actions—loan modifications, trial-period plans, and payment plans—during the fourth quarter of 2013. The number of home retention actions decreased 22.4 percent from the previous quarter and 34.0 percent from a year earlier. Servicers implemented 72,466 modifications, a decrease of 49.5 percent from a year earlier. New HAMP modifications decreased 10.1 percent to 20,829 during the quarter and other modifications decreased 32.2 percent to 51,637. Servicers implemented 82,269 new trial-period plans, a decrease of 18.7 percent from the previous quarter and 32.4 percent from a year earlier. New payment plans decreased by 21.7 percent from the previous quarter to 88,093. During the past five quarters, servicers initiated 1.6 million home retention actions—561,998 modifications, 509,315 trial-period plans, and 517,623 payment plans.

Table 13. Number of New Home Retention Actions							
	12/31/12	3/31/13	6/30/13	9/30/13	12/31/13	1Q %Change	1Y %Change
Other Modifications	114,181	110,519	85,582	76,134	51,637	-32.2%	-54.8%
HAMP Modifications	29,314	28,030	22,613	23,159	20,829	-10.1%	-28.9%
Other Trial-Period Plans	96,424	85,516	68,465	62,163	50,743	-18.4%	-47.4%
HAMP Trial-Period Plans	25,306	18,145	32,028	38,999	31,526	-19.2%	24.6%
Payment Plans	102,446	107,113	107,403	112,568	88,093	-21.7%	-14.0%
Total	367,671	349,323	316,091	313,023	242,828	-22.4%	-34.0%

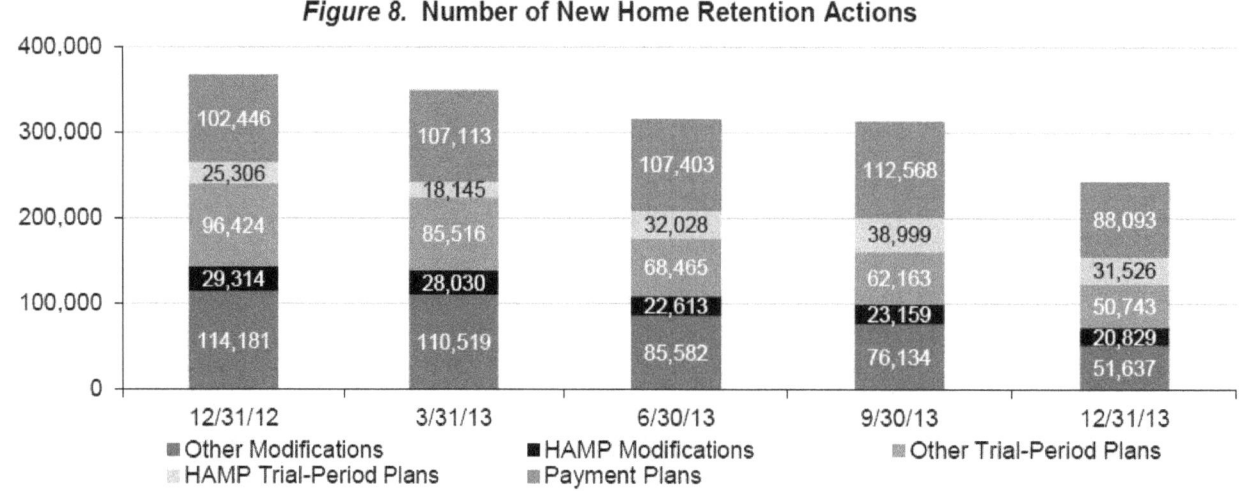

Figure 8. Number of New Home Retention Actions

HAMP Modifications and Trial-Period Plans, by Investor and Risk Category

Of the 20,829 HAMP modifications implemented during the fourth quarter of 2013, GSE mortgages received 21.6 percent, government-guaranteed loans received 31.6 percent, loans held in portfolio received 25.3 percent, and loans serviced for private investors received 21.4 percent. Prime mortgages represented about 75 percent of the total portfolio and received 40.6 percent of all HAMP modifications. Subprime loans represented about 6 percent of the total portfolio and received 25.2 percent of HAMP modifications during the quarter.

Table 14. HAMP Modifications, by Investor and Risk Category (Modifications Implemented in the Fourth Quarter of 2013)						
	Fannie Mae	Freddie Mac	Government-Guaranteed	Portfolio	Private	Total
Prime	1,115	1,429	1,628	2,342	1,941	8,455
Alt-A	308	422	2,145	1,224	981	5,080
Subprime	246	245	1,955	1,558	1,254	5,258
Other	501	242	856	154	283	2,036
Total	2,170	2,338	6,584	5,278	4,459	20,829

Servicers implemented 31,526 HAMP trial-period plans during the quarter, an increase of 24.6 percent from a year earlier. GSE mortgages received 12.3 percent of HAMP trial-period plans initiated during the quarter, government-guaranteed loans received 66.8 percent, loans held in portfolio received 8.0 percent, and loans serviced for private investors received 12.9 percent. Prime mortgages received 31.6 percent of the HAMP trial-period plans implemented during the quarter, Alt-A loans received 29.5 percent, and subprime and other mortgages collectively received 38.9 percent.

Table 15. HAMP Trial-Period Plans, by Investor and Risk Category (Trial-Period Plans Implemented in the Fourth Quarter of 2013)						
	Fannie Mae	Freddie Mac	Government-Guaranteed	Portfolio	Private	Total
Prime	970	1,212	5,089	1,034	1,656	9,961
Alt-A	297	344	7,190	534	924	9,289
Subprime	200	219	5,359	681	1,154	7,613
Other	445	195	3,419	277	327	4,663
Total	1,912	1,970	21,057	2,526	4,061	31,526

New Home Retention Actions Relative to Newly Initiated Foreclosures

Servicers continued to implement more home retention actions than new foreclosures during the quarter. The ratio of new home retention actions to newly initiated foreclosures decreased 16.8 percent from a year earlier. Although the number of new home retention actions and new foreclosures both decreased from the previous quarter and a year earlier, new retention activity fell more than the new foreclosures.

Table 16. Percentage of New Home Retention Actions Relative to Newly Initiated Foreclosures, by Risk Category							
	12/31/12	3/31/13	6/30/13	9/30/13	12/31/13	1Q %Change	1Y %Change
Prime	254.9%	216.0%	222.7%	246.8%	199.8%	-19.1%	-21.6%
Alt-A	242.4%	198.1%	216.6%	252.8%	209.6%	-17.1%	-13.5%
Subprime	256.9%	204.2%	212.6%	242.4%	190.1%	-21.5%	-26.0%
Other	150.1%	133.1%	163.9%	199.4%	169.3%	15.1%	12.8%
Overall	234.5%	195.9%	209.9%	239.7%	195.1%	-18.6%	-16.8%
Number of New Home Retention Actions	367,671	349,323	316,091	313,023	242,828	-22.4%	-34.0%
Number of Newly Initiated Foreclosures	156,773	178,360	150,592	130,592	124,468	-4.7%	-20.6%

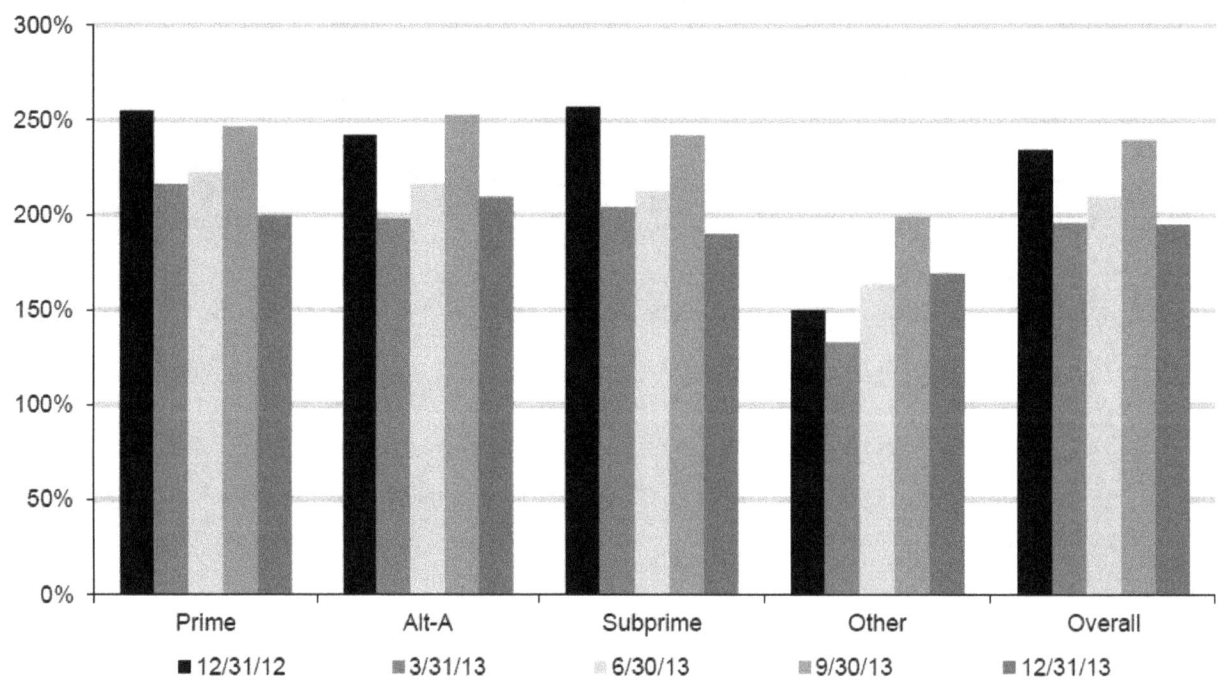

Figure 9. New Home Retention Actions Relative to Newly Initiated Foreclosures, by Risk Category

Types of Modification Actions

The types of modification actions or combinations of actions have different effects on the borrowers' mortgages and their monthly principal and interest payments. Different actions may have different effects on the long-term sustainability of mortgages. Servicers often use a combination of actions when modifying mortgages, with 95.3 percent of modifications implemented during the fourth quarter of 2013 changing more than one of the original loan terms. Capitalization, interest-rate reduction and term extension remain the primary actions used in modifying mortgages.

Servicers capitalized missed fees and payments in 87.2 percent of modifications implemented during the quarter, reduced interest rates in 76.7 percent, and extended loan maturity in 75.9 percent. Servicers reduced some portion of the unpaid principal in 10.5 percent of modifications completed during the quarter, a decrease of 22.5 percent from the previous quarter and 47.4 percent from a year earlier. Servicers deferred repayment of some portion of the unpaid principal in 30.6 percent of modifications made during the quarter, up 49.3 percent from a year earlier. Because most modifications changed more than one term, the sum of the individual actions exceeded 100 percent of total modifications. Appendix D presents additional detail on combination modifications.

Table 17. Changes in Loan Terms for Modifications Through the Fourth Quarter of 2013							
(Percentage of Total Modifications in Each Category)							
	12/31/12	3/31/13	6/30/13	9/30/13	12/31/13	1Q %Change	1Y %Change
Capitalization	84.6%	79.3%	81.7%	83.6%	87.2%	4.3%	3.0%
Rate Reduction	73.3%	80.1%	81.0%	78.9%	76.7%	-2.8%	4.7%
Rate Freeze	3.9%	3.7%	5.2%	5.5%	7.0%	28.4%	77.9%
Term Extension	58.9%	60.3%	67.7%	69.3%	75.9%	9.6%	28.9%
Principal Reduction	20.0%	15.2%	12.2%	13.6%	10.5%	-22.5%	-47.4%
Principal Deferral	20.5%	18.2%	20.5%	25.3%	30.6%	20.9%	49.3%
Not Reported*	1.1%	0.6%	1.4%	2.2%	0.7%	-68.1%	-37.8%
(Number of Changes in Each Category)							
Capitalization	121,454	109,882	88,418	82,998	63,169	-23.9%	-48.0%
Rate Reduction	105,115	110,910	87,639	78,309	55,554	-29.1%	-47.1%
Rate Freeze	5,644	5,121	5,619	5,413	5,072	-6.3%	-10.1%
Term Extension	84,518	83,594	73,254	68,820	55,026	-20.0%	-34.9%
Principal Reduction	28,765	21,033	13,150	13,502	7,634	-43.5%	-73.5%
Principal Deferral	29,445	25,272	22,195	25,150	22,195	-11.7%	-24.6%
Not Reported*	1,599	900	1,496	2,155	502	-76.7%	-68.6%

*Processing constraints at some servicers prevented them from reporting specific modified term(s).

Types of HAMP Modification Actions

Consistent with modification actions overall and the prescribed order of actions required by the program, HAMP modifications most often included capitalization of missed payments and fees, interest-rate reductions, and term extensions. Servicers used capitalization in 69.5 percent of modifications, down from 92.0 percent a year ago. Servicers used principal deferral, another prescribed action in HAMP, in 26.3 percent of HAMP modifications during the fourth quarter of 2013, down from 29.2 percent a year earlier. Servicers used principal reduction in 15.6 percent of HAMP modifications implemented during the quarter—a decrease of 28.3 percent from the previous quarter and 37.8 percent from a year earlier, when 25.1 percent of HAMP modifications included principal reduction.

Table 18. Changes in Loan Terms for HAMP Modifications Through the Fourth Quarter of 2013 (Percentage of Total Modifications in Each Category)							
	12/31/12	3/31/13	6/30/13	9/30/13	12/31/13	1Q %Change	1Y %Change
Capitalization	92.0%	95.1%	88.6%	90.3%	69.5%	-23.1%	-24.5%
Rate Reduction	81.3%	84.9%	88.8%	88.9%	90.3%	1.6%	11.0%
Rate Freeze	4.0%	3.5%	2.6%	3.1%	2.4%	-23.9%	-40.0%
Term Extension	53.0%	53.8%	57.6%	60.1%	74.1%	23.4%	39.9%
Principal Reduction	25.1%	22.3%	20.0%	21.8%	15.6%	-28.3%	-37.8%
Principal Deferral	29.2%	31.9%	36.2%	35.0%	26.3%	-24.9%	-10.1%
Not Reported*	1.7%	0.2%	0.4%	1.2%	0.3%	-72.8%	-81.2%
(Number of Changes in Each Category)							
Capitalization	26,981	26,646	20,039	20,920	14,475	-30.8%	-46.4%
Rate Reduction	23,844	23,790	20,072	20,589	18,808	-8.7%	-21.1%
Rate Freeze	1,171	981	582	729	499	-31.6%	-57.4%
Term Extension	15,532	15,089	13,032	13,913	15,437	11.0%	-0.6%
Principal Reduction	7,353	6,245	4,527	5,046	3,252	-35.6%	-55.8%
Principal Deferral	8,570	8,930	8,176	8,103	5,475	-32.4%	-36.1%
Not Reported*	508	50	83	278	68	-75.5%	-86.6%

*Processing constraints at some servicers prevented them from reporting specific modified term(s).

Types of Modification Actions, by Risk Category

Servicers use a combination of actions when modifying mortgages. Modifications across all risk categories predominantly featured interest-rate reduction and term extension in addition to the capitalization of past-due interest and fees. Because most modifications changed more than one term, the sum of individual features changed exceeded the total number of modified loans in each risk category. While most actions were used relatively consistently across all risk categories, servicers used principal deferral less frequently and principal reduction more frequently for subprime loans than for other risk classes. Servicers also used term extensions less frequently for subprime loans than for other risk categories.

Table 19. Changes in Loan Terms for Modifications, by Risk Category, During the Fourth Quarter of 2013 (Percentage of Total Modifications in Each Category)					
	Prime	Alt-A	Subprime	Other	Overall
Capitalization	89.4%	83.9%	86.8%	86.3%	87.2%
Rate Reduction	77.1%	78.0%	75.6%	75.0%	76.7%
Rate Freeze	6.6%	5.8%	6.5%	11.3%	7.0%
Term Extension	76.1%	76.7%	69.6%	85.3%	75.9%
Principal Reduction	10.6%	10.9%	15.0%	1.7%	10.5%
Principal Deferral	31.0%	31.1%	27.9%	33.5%	30.6%
Not Reported*	0.8%	0.6%	0.6%	0.5%	0.7%
(Number of Changes in Each Category)					
Total Mortgages Modified	30,690	16,244	16,295	9,237	72,466
Capitalization	27,432	13,621	14,146	7,970	63,169
Rate Reduction	23,647	12,664	12,315	6,928	55,554
Rate Freeze	2,022	941	1,065	1,044	5,072
Term Extension	23,341	12,462	11,344	7,879	55,026
Principal Reduction	3,259	1,772	2,444	159	7,634
Principal Deferral	9,515	5,048	4,541	3,091	22,195
Not Reported*	257	102	95	48	502

*Processing constraints at some servicers prevented them from reporting specific modified term(s).

Types of Modification Actions, by Investor and Product Type

Modifications of mortgages serviced for the GSEs accounted for 39.4 percent of all modifications made during the fourth quarter of 2013. Government-guaranteed loans received 24.6 percent of all modifications, mortgages serviced for private investors received 18.6 percent, and mortgages held in the servicers' own portfolios received 17.4 percent of all fourth-quarter modifications. Interest-rate reduction, capitalization of missed payments and fees, and term extension remained the primary types of modification actions. Servicers used principal reduction most frequently in modifying loans held in portfolio or serviced for private investors because Fannie Mae and Freddie Mac do not allow principal reduction. Because modifications often change more than one loan term, the sum of the actions exceeded the number of modified loans for each investor.

Table 20. Type of Modification Action, by Investor and Product Type, During the Fourth Quarter of 2013
(Percentage of Total Modifications in Each Category)

	Fannie Mae	Freddie Mac	Government-Guaranteed	Private Investor	Portfolio	Overall
Capitalization	96.3%	97.5%	61.9%	93.6%	94.2%	87.2%
Rate Reduction	61.6%	79.5%	91.0%	73.6%	75.0%	76.7%
Rate Freeze	14.3%	3.9%	3.2%	4.6%	9.2%	7.0%
Term Extension	92.1%	94.4%	94.8%	26.6%	62.9%	75.9%
Principal Reduction	0.4%	0.2%	0.2%	19.9%	38.4%	10.5%
Principal Deferral	24.0%	34.2%	35.0%	33.3%	25.9%	30.6%
Not Reported*	1.5%	0.2%	0.3%	1.1%	0.5%	0.7%
(Number of Changes in Each Category)						
Total Mortgages Modified	15,368	13,184	17,854	13,461	12,599	72,466
Capitalization	14,796	12,852	11,049	12,604	11,868	63,169
Rate Reduction	9,474	10,484	16,249	9,902	9,445	55,554
Rate Freeze	2,197	517	579	623	1,156	5,072
Term Extension	14,151	12,444	16,924	3,578	7,929	55,026
Principal Reduction	61	21	39	2,676	4,837	7,634
Principal Deferral	3,685	4,514	6,254	4,476	3,266	22,195
Not Reported	226	21	50	148	57	502

*Processing constraints at some servicers prevented them from reporting specific modified term(s).

**The principal reduction actions reported for Fannie Mae and Freddie Mac mortgages in this table represent coding errors to be corrected in subsequent reporting periods.

Types of HAMP Modification Actions, by Investor and Product Type

Of the 20,829 HAMP modifications implemented in the fourth quarter of 2013, 21.6 percent were on GSE mortgages, 31.6 percent were on government-guaranteed loans, 21.4 percent were on mortgages serviced for private investors, and 25.3 percent were on mortgages held in servicers' portfolios. Consistent with total modification actions, the prevailing actions among HAMP modifications were capitalization of past-due interest and fees, interest-rate reduction, and term extension. Servicers used principal deferral in a significant number of HAMP modifications for all investors other than government-guaranteed loans. Principal reduction was concentrated in loans held in portfolio and serviced for private investors. Almost 52 percent of the HAMP modifications completed during the fourth quarter of 2013 on loans held in the banks' own portfolios included a principal reduction.

Table 21. Type of HAMP Modification Action, by Investor and Product Type, During the Fourth Quarter of 2013

(Percentage of Total Modifications in Each Category)	Fannie Mae	Freddie Mac	Government-Guaranteed	Private Investor	Portfolio	Overall
Capitalization	95.9%	97.7%	9.3%	97.5%	97.6%	69.5%
Rate Reduction	95.3%	99.4%	95.6%	83.6%	83.3%	90.3%
Rate Freeze	1.6%	0.9%	0.5%	3.7%	4.5%	2.4%
Term Extension	71.5%	74.6%	99.5%	35.1%	76.4%	74.1%
Principal Reduction	0.2%	0.0%	0.2%	11.2%	51.9%	15.6%
Principal Deferral	28.8%	30.5%	0.3%	55.2%	31.4%	26.3%
Not Reported*	2.0%	0.4%	0.2%	0.0%	0.1%	0.3%
(Number of Changes in Each Category)						
Total Mortgages Modified	2,170	2,338	6,584	4,459	5,278	20,829
Capitalization	2,081	2,284	613	4,348	5,149	14,475
Rate Reduction	2,067	2,323	6,295	3,726	4,397	18,808
Rate Freeze	34	22	36	167	240	499
Term Extension	1,551	1,743	6,548	1,565	4,030	15,437
Principal Reduction**	4	0	10	499	2,739	3,252
Principal Deferral	625	714	18	2,462	1,656	5,475
Not Reported	43	10	10	0	5	68

*Processing constraints at some servicers prevented them from reporting specific modified term(s).

**The principal reduction actions reported for Fannie Mae mortgages in this table represent coding errors to be corrected in subsequent reporting periods.

Changes in Monthly Payments Resulting From Modification

The previous sections of this report describe the types of modification actions across risk categories, investors, and product types. This section describes the effect of those changes on borrowers' monthly principal and interest payments.

Modifications that decrease payments occur when servicers elect to lower interest rates, extend the amortization period, or defer or forgive principal. The reduced payments can make mortgages more affordable to borrowers and more sustainable over time. The lower payments, however, also result in less monthly cash flow and interest income to mortgage investors.

Mortgage modifications may increase monthly payments when borrowers and servicers agree to add past-due interest, advances for taxes or insurance, and other fees to the loan balances and re-amortize the new balances over the remaining life of the mortgages. The interest rate or maturity of the loans may be changed on these modifications but not enough to offset the increase in payments caused by the additional capitalized principal. Modifications may also result in increased monthly payments when interest rates or principal payments on ARMs and payment-option ARMs are reset higher but by less than the amount indicated in the original mortgage contracts.

Modifications that increase payments may be appropriate when borrowers resolve temporary problems with cash flow, or otherwise have reasonable prospects of making higher payments to repay the debt over time. This strategy carries additional risk, however, especially during periods of prolonged economic stress, underscoring the importance of verifying borrowers' income and debt-payment ability so that borrowers and servicers have confidence that the modifications will be sustainable.

Servicers also modify some mortgage contracts by simply leaving principal and interest payments unchanged. This occurs, for example, when servicers freeze current interest rates and payments instead of allowing them to increase to levels required by the original mortgage contracts.

Changes in Monthly Payments Resulting From Modifications, by Quarter

Ninety-one percent of modifications made in the quarter reduced monthly principal and interest payments and 64.6 percent of the modifications reduced payments by 20 percent or more.

Table 22. Changes in Monthly Principal and Interest Payments Resulting From Modifications (Percentage of Modifications in Each Category)*							
	12/31/12	3/31/13	6/30/13	9/30/13	12/31/13	1Q %Change	1Y %Change
Decreased by 20% or More	58.9%	56.4%	59.2%	62.5%	64.6%	3.3%	9.7%
Decreased by 10% to Less Than 20%	21.0%	24.1%	21.4%	18.8%	16.9%	-10.3%	-19.8%
Decreased by Less Than 10%	13.4%	13.2%	12.4%	11.1%	9.5%	-14.0%	-28.9%
Subtotal for Decreased	**93.4%**	**93.7%**	**93.0%**	**92.4%**	**91.0%**	**-1.5%**	**-2.5%**
Unchanged	1.0%	0.9%	1.0%	0.8%	1.3%	62.0%	31.8%
Increased	5.7%	5.4%	6.0%	6.8%	7.7%	13.7%	36.2%
Subtotal for Unchanged and Increased	**6.6%**	**6.3%**	**7.0%**	**7.6%**	**9.0%**	**18.8%**	**35.5%**
Total	100.0%	100.0%	100.0%	100.0%	100.0%		
(Number of Modifications in Each Category)							
Decreased by 20% or More	84,103	77,674	63,515	61,308	46,511	-24.1%	-44.7%
Decreased by 10% to Less Than 20%	30,056	33,143	23,005	18,443	12,154	-34.1%	-59.6%
Decreased by Less Than 10%	19,169	18,187	13,323	10,876	6,872	-36.8%	-64.2%
Subtotal for Decreased	**133,328**	**129,004**	**99,843**	**90,627**	**65,537**	**-27.7%**	**-50.8%**
Unchanged	1,404	1,229	1,124	784	933	19.0%	-33.5%
Increased	8,080	7,389	6,405	6,643	5,550	-16.5%	-31.3%
Subtotal for Unchanged and Increased	**9,484**	**8,618**	**7,529**	**7,427**	**6,483**	**-12.7%**	**-31.6%**
Total	142,812	137,622	107,372	98,054	72,020	-26.6%	-49.6%

* No payment change information was reported on 683 modifications in the fourth quarter of 2012, 927 in the first quarter of 2013, 823 in the second quarter of 2013, 1,239 in the third quarter of 2013, and 446 in the fourth quarter of 2013.

Figure 10. Changes in Monthly Principal and Interest Payments
Percentage of Modifications in Each Category

■ Increased ▪ Unchanged ▪ Decreased

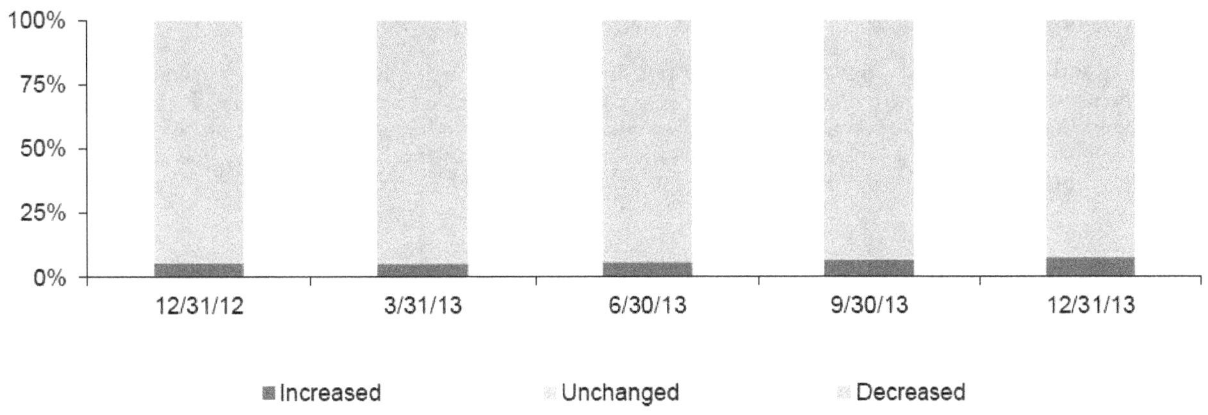

Changes in Monthly Payments Resulting From HAMP Modifications, by Quarter

More than 98 percent of HAMP modifications completed during the fourth quarter of 2013 reduced borrower monthly payments, with 73.7 percent reducing payments by 20 percent or more. In addition to achieving lower payments, HAMP attempts to increase payment sustainability by targeting monthly payments at 31 percent of borrowers' income. Performance data on all modifications show that re-default rates are lowest among loans that receive at least a 10 percent reduction in their monthly payments, and that the greater the decrease in payment, the lower the rate of re-default.

Table 23. Changes in Monthly Principal and Interest Payments Resulting From HAMP Modifications (Percentage of HAMP Modifications in Each Category)*/**							
	12/31/12	3/31/13	6/30/13	9/30/13	12/31/13	1Q %Change	1Y %Change
Decreased by 20% or More	76.8%	76.3%	77.8%	76.8%	73.7%	-4.0%	-4.0%
Decreased by 10% to Less Than 20%	13.0%	13.1%	12.3%	13.4%	17.1%	27.8%	31.6%
Decreased by Less Than 10%	8.4%	8.5%	7.4%	7.9%	7.3%	-7.9%	-13.9%
Subtotal for Decreased	**98.3%**	**98.0%**	**97.5%**	**98.1%**	**98.1%**	**0.0%**	**-0.1%**
Unchanged	0.3%	0.5%	0.9%	0.1%	0.1%	-18.4%	-54.3%
Increased	1.5%	1.5%	1.6%	1.8%	1.8%	-1.1%	19.2%
Subtotal for Unchanged and Increased	**1.7%**	**2.0%**	**2.5%**	**1.9%**	**1.9%**	**-2.5%**	**8.1%**
Total	100.0%	100.0%	100.0%	100.0%	100.0%		
(Number of HAMP Modifications in Each Category)							
Decreased by 20% or More	22,458	21,321	17,527	17,705	15,316	-13.5%	-31.8%
Decreased by 10% to Less Than 20%	3,801	3,672	2,768	3,088	3,554	15.1%	-6.5%
Decreased by Less Than 10%	2,465	2,389	1,671	1,817	1,508	-17.0%	-38.8%
Subtotal for Decreased	**28,724**	**27,382**	**21,966**	**22,610**	**20,378**	**-9.9%**	**-29.1%**
Unchanged	77	138	205	34	25	-26.5%	-67.5%
Increased	432	431	363	411	366	-10.9%	-15.3%
Subtotal for Unchanged and Increased	**509**	**569**	**568**	**445**	**391**	**-12.1%**	**-23.2%**
Total	29,233	27,951	22,534	23,055	20,769	-9.9%	-29.0%

*No payment change information was reported on 81 modifications in the fourth quarter of 2012, 79 in the first quarter, 79 in the second quarter, 104 in the third quarter, and 60 in the fourth quarter of 2013.

**Some HAMP modifications, like other modifications, may increase the borrowers' monthly principal and interest payments when loans with a previous interest-only or partial payment are modified to amortize the loans over their remaining terms, or when ARMs are reset to higher rates and payments but at lower rates than otherwise contractually required. While the principal and interest portion of the payment might increase, the total payment will reflect a target housing expense ratio of 31 percent as specified by HAMP.

Average Change in Monthly Payments Resulting From Modifications, by Quarter

Modifications made during the fourth quarter of 2013 reduced monthly principal and interest payments by $344, or 26.6 percent, on average. HAMP modifications made during the quarter reduced payments by $422, or 31.5 percent, on average. Other modifications reduced payments by $313, or 24.5 percent, on average. The decrease in the average reduction in monthly payments can be attributed to the lower average balance of mortgages receiving modifications.

Table 24. Average Change in Monthly Payments Resulting From Modifications, by Quarter*							
All Modifications							
	12/31/12	3/31/13	6/30/13	9/30/13	12/31/13	1Q %Change	1Y %Change
Decreased by 20% or More	(594)	(560)	(545)	(535)	(498)	-7.0%	-16.2%
Decreased by 10% to Less Than 20%	(189)	(186)	(172)	(176)	(172)	-2.4%	-8.7%
Decreased by Less Than 10%	(68)	(71)	(68)	(67)	(68)	0.4%	-0.5%
Unchanged	0	0	0	0	0		
Increased**	169	166	159	159	161	1.0%	-4.8%
Overall (in dollars)	(389)	(361)	(358)	(365)	(344)	-5.5%	-11.4%
Percentage Change	-25.8%	-25.2%	-25.9%	-26.6%	-26.6%		
Other Modifications							
Decreased by 20% or More	(560)	(516)	(503)	(492)	(483)	-1.8%	-13.7%
Decreased by 10% to Less Than 20%	(186)	(183)	(167)	(170)	(171)	0.1%	-8.2%
Decreased by Less Than 10%	(67)	(70)	(66)	(65)	(66)	0.8%	-1.2%
Unchanged	0	0	0	0	0		
Increased**	168	165	158	158	161	1.9%	-3.8%
Overall (in dollars)	(345)	(314)	(311)	(316)	(313)	-0.8%	-9.3%
Percentage Change	-23.4%	-22.7%	-23.4%	-24.2%	-24.5%		
HAMP Modifications							
Decreased by 20% or More	(687)	(677)	(654)	(642)	(527)	-17.9%	-23.2%
Decreased by 10% to Less Than 20%	(208)	(212)	(211)	(207)	(176)	-14.8%	-15.3%
Decreased by Less Than 10%	(78)	(77)	(79)	(78)	(74)	-4.4%	-4.4%
Unchanged	0	0	0	0	0		
Increased**	191	193	183	171	152	-11.1%	-20.1%
Overall (in dollars)	(558)	(548)	(538)	(524)	(422)	-19.5%	-24.5%
Percentage Change	-35.4%	-35.0%	-35.1%	-34.6%	-31.5%		

*Parentheses indicate that, on average, borrowers' monthly payments decreased by the amount enclosed within the parentheses.

**Some modifications may increase the borrowers' monthly principal and interest payments when past-due interest, advances for taxes or insurance, and other fees are added to loan balances. The monthly payments may also increase when loans with a previous interest-only or partial payment are modified to amortize the loans over their remaining terms.

B. Modified Loan Performance

Re-Default Rates of Modified Loans: 60 or More Days Delinquent

Modification performance may vary because of many factors, including the types of modification actions, the average amount of change in the borrower's monthly payment, the characteristics and geographic location of the modified loans, and the addition or deletion of modification programs among the reporting institutions. Despite differences in many of these factors, mortgages modified in each of the last five quarters have performed similarly over time. Among modifications completed in each of the last five quarters, between 5.8 percent and 9.0 percent of the modified loans were 60 or more days delinquent three months after modification, 11.5 percent to 13.6 percent were 60 or more days delinquent six months after modification, and 18.5 percent to 18.8 percent were 60 or more days delinquent 12 months after modification.

Table 25. Modified Loans 60 or More Days Delinquent					
Modification Date*	3 Months After Modification	6 Months After Modification	9 Months After Modification	12 Months After Modification	15 Months After Modification
Third Quarter 2012	7.2%	13.0%	15.9%	18.8%	21.1%
Fourth Quarter 2012	7.3%	11.5%	15.7%	18.5%	-
First Quarter 2013	5.8%	11.6%	15.9%	-	-
Second Quarter 2013	7.2%	13.6%	-	-	-
Third Quarter 2013	9.0%	-	-	-	-

*All re-default data are based on modified loans that remain in effect at the specified amount of time after the modification. All loans that have been repaid in full, been refinanced, been sold, or completed the foreclosure process are removed from the calculation. Data include only modifications that have had time to age the indicated number of months.

Figure 11. Modified Loans 60 or More Days Delinquent

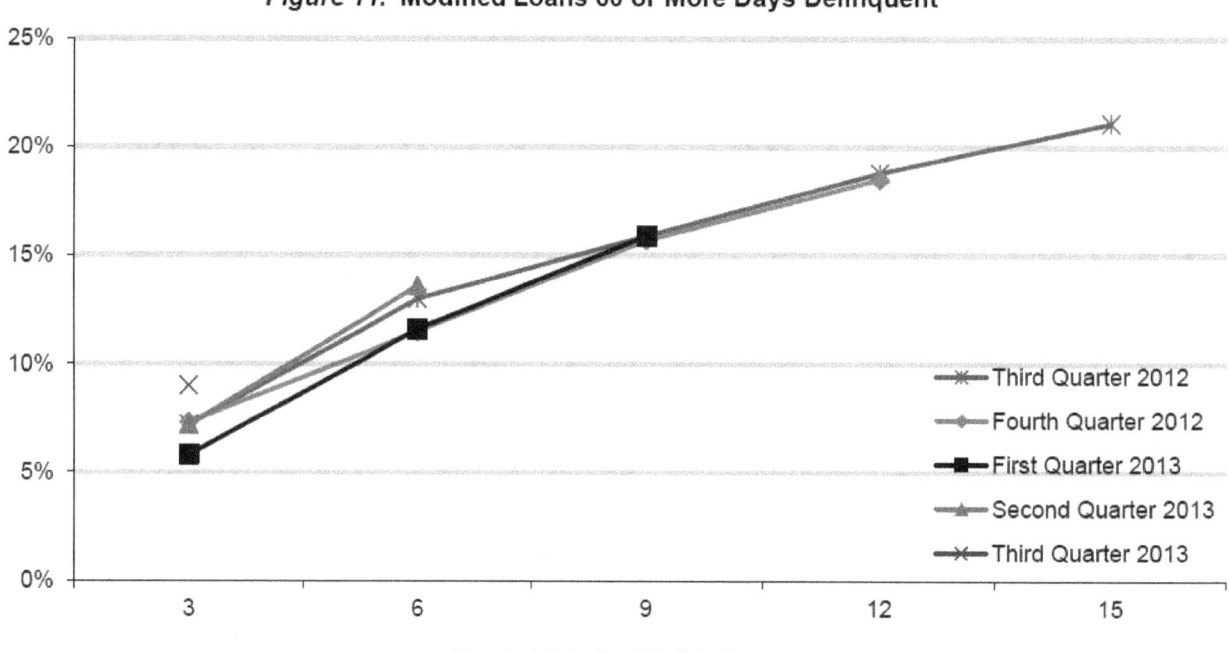

*Data for the third quarter of 2013 is a single point (9.0 percent).

Re-Default Rates of Modified Loans: 30 or More Days Delinquent

Re-default rates measured at 30 or more days delinquent provide an early indicator of mortgages that may need additional attention to prevent more serious delinquency or foreclosure. For modifications completed in each of the last five quarters, 14.2 percent to 19.1 percent were 30 or more days delinquent three months after modification. Among modifications outstanding at least one year, 28.5 percent to 29.0 percent were 30 or more days delinquent.

Table 26. Modified Loans 30 or More Days Delinquent					
Modification Date*	3 Months After Modification	6 Months After Modification	9 Months After Modification	12 Months After Modification	15 Months After Modification
Third Quarter 2012	16.5%	22.7%	25.6%	29.0%	30.9%
Fourth Quarter 2012	16.3%	21.3%	26.1%	28.5%	-
First Quarter 2013	14.2%	22.1%	26.2%	-	-
Second Quarter 2013	17.4%	24.9%	-	-	-
Third Quarter 2013	19.1%	-	-	-	-

*Data include only modifications that have had time to age the indicated number of months.

Figure 12. Modified Loans 30 or More Days Delinquent

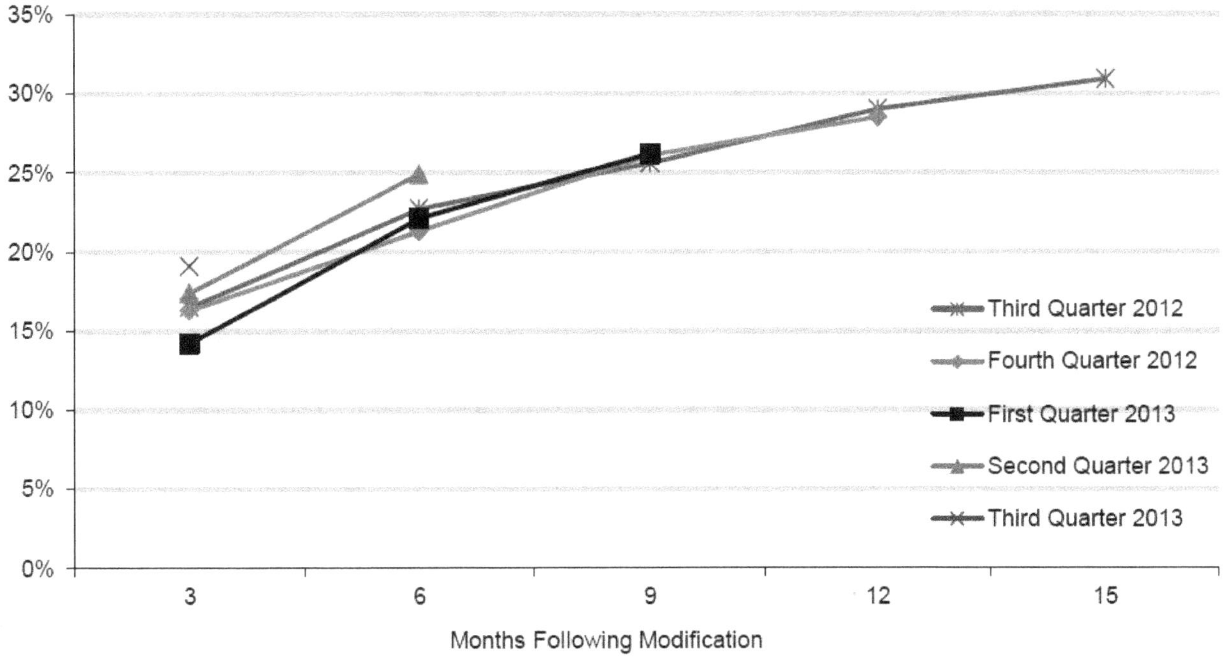

*Data for the third quarter of 2013 is a single point (19.1 percent).

Re-Default Rates of Modified Loans: 90 or More Days Delinquent

Among modifications completed during the last five quarters, less than 14 percent were 90 or more days delinquent 12 months after modification.

Table 27. Modified Loans 90 or More Days Delinquent*					
Modification Date*	3 Months After Modification	6 Months After Modification	9 Months After Modification	12 Months After Modification	15 Months After Modification
Third Quarter 2012	3.1%	8.2%	11.1%	13.7%	16.0%
Fourth Quarter 2012	3.7%	7.1%	10.7%	13.4%	-
First Quarter 2013	2.7%	6.9%	10.6%	-	-
Second Quarter 2013	3.2%	8.3%	-	-	-
Third Quarter 2013	4.8%	-	-	-	-

*Data include only modifications that have had time to age the indicated number of months.

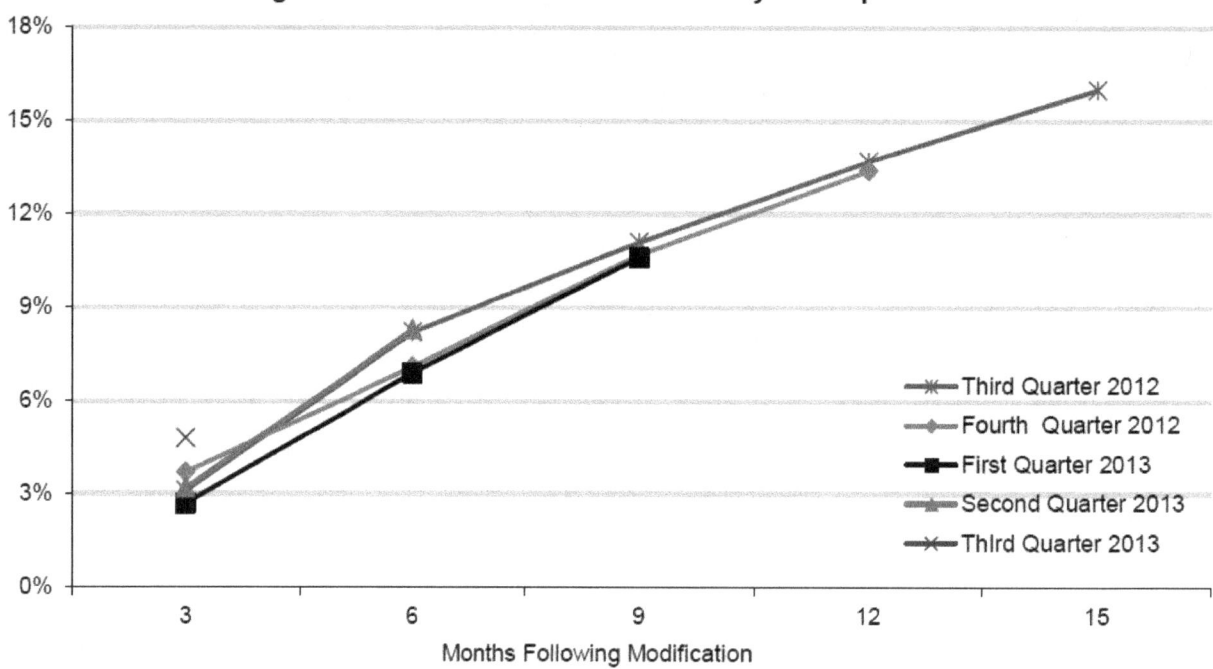

Figure 13. Modified Loans 90 or More Days Delinquent

*Data for the third quarter of 2013 is a single point (4.8 percent).

Re-Default Rate, by Investor (60 or More Days Delinquent)

Modifications on mortgages held in the servicers' own portfolios or serviced for the GSEs—Fannie Mae and Freddie Mac—performed better than modifications on mortgages serviced for other investors. These lower re-default rates for portfolio and GSE mortgages may reflect differences in loan risk characteristics and modification programs, and additional flexibility to modify terms of portfolio mortgages for greater sustainability. Re-default rates for government-guaranteed mortgages and loans serviced for private investors were highest over time, reflecting the higher risk characteristics associated with those mortgages. For all investors, re-default rates generally have decreased over time as more recent modifications have focused more on reducing monthly payments and increasing borrowers' ability to sustain the reduced payments over time and as the housing market and broader economy have continued their recovery.

Table 28. Re-Default Rates for Portfolio Loans and Loans Serviced for Others Modified in 2008 (60 or More Days Delinquent)					
Investor Loan Type	6 Months After Modification	12 Months After Modification	18 Months After Modification	24 Months After Modification	36 Months After Modification
Fannie Mae	45.2%	59.7%	63.9%	62.1%	54.4%
Freddie Mac	45.0%	59.2%	64.4%	64.6%	59.5%
Government-Guaranteed	53.6%	67.8%	70.8%	70.3%	67.7%
Private	49.1%	61.2%	66.7%	68.0%	68.2%
Portfolio Loans	25.2%	36.2%	41.0%	41.7%	40.1%
Overall	44.8%	57.2%	62.1%	62.7%	61.4%

Table 29. Re-Default Rates for Portfolio Loans and Loans Serviced for Others Modified in 2009 (60 or More Days Delinquent)					
Investor Loan Type	6 Months After Modification	12 Months After Modification	18 Months After Modification	24 Months After Modification	36 Months After Modification
Fannie Mae	31.3%	41.1%	42.5%	42.4%	39.1%
Freddie Mac	37.3%	44.8%	46.0%	44.9%	40.1%
Government-Guaranteed	42.1%	55.6%	56.4%	56.3%	58.6%
Private	40.8%	52.5%	56.8%	57.8%	54.4%
Portfolio Loans	15.4%	24.9%	29.6%	30.6%	30.2%
Overall	32.2%	43.2%	46.4%	46.9%	45.1%

Table 30. Re-Default Rates for Portfolio Loans and Loans Serviced for Others Modified in 2010 (60 or More Days Delinquent)*					
Investor Loan Type	6 Months After Modification	12 Months After Modification	18 Months After Modification	24 Months After Modification	36 Months After Modification
Fannie Mae	14.2%	20.6%	23.9%	24.3%	23.2%
Freddie Mac	12.1%	17.8%	20.7%	21.9%	20.8%
Government-Guaranteed	27.4%	40.7%	46.6%	48.8%	49.1%
Private	19.8%	28.3%	33.2%	33.7%	29.0%
Portfolio Loans	11.7%	18.0%	20.9%	22.0%	20.9%
Overall	17.3%	25.4%	29.5%	30.6%	29.2%

Table 31. Re-Default Rates for Portfolio Loans and Loans Serviced for Others Modified in 2011
(60 or More Days Delinquent)*

Investor Loan Type	6 Months After Modification	12 Months After Modification	18 Months After Modification	24 Months After Modification	36 Months After Modification
Fannie Mae	11.2%	16.7%	18.9%	20.4%	-
Freddie Mac	10.9%	16.8%	20.1%	19.3%	-
Government-Guaranteed	28.0%	42.3%	47.9%	48.1%	-
Private	15.5%	22.1%	24.5%	21.5%	-
Portfolio Loans	9.3%	15.1%	18.1%	18.1%	-
Overall	15.4%	23.2%	26.6%	26.4%	-

Table 32. Re-Default Rates for Portfolio Loans and Loans Serviced for Others Modified in 2012
(60 or More Days Delinquent)*

Investor Loan Type	6 Months After Modification	12 Months After Modification	18 Months After Modification	24 Months After Modification	36 Months After Modification
Fannie Mae	11.5%	16.9%	21.0%	-	-
Freddie Mac	8.8%	12.9%	14.1%	-	-
Government-Guaranteed	21.3%	33.4%	39.7%	-	-
Private	13.0%	16.8%	17.0%	-	-
Portfolio Loans	7.2%	11.1%	14.9%	-	-
Overall	12.7%	18.8%	21.2%	-	-

Table 33. Re-Default Rates for Portfolio Loans and Loans Serviced for Others Modified in 2013
(60 or More Days Delinquent)*

Investor Loan Type	6 Months After Modification	12 Months After Modification	18 Months After Modification	24 Months After Modification	36 Months After Modification
Fannie Mae	11.8%	-	-	-	-
Freddie Mac	8.6%	-	-	-	-
Government-Guaranteed	18.2%	-	-	-	-
Private	11.8%	-	-	-	-
Portfolio Loans	7.1%	-	-	-	-
Overall	12.5%	-	-	-	-

*Data in tables 30-33 include modifications that were originated that year and aged the indicated number of months.

Performance of HAMP Modifications Compared With Other Modifications

HAMP modifications have performed better than other modifications implemented during the same periods. These lower post-modification delinquency rates reflect HAMP's emphasis on the affordability of monthly payments relative to the borrower's income, verification of income, and completion of a successful trial-payment period. While these criteria result in better performance of HAMP modifications over time, the greater flexibility in making other types of modifications results in more of those modifications for borrowers who do not qualify for HAMP modifications.

Table 34. Performance of HAMP Modifications Compared With Other Modifications (60 or More Days Delinquent)*						
	Number of Modifications	3 Months After Modification	6 Months After Modification	9 Months After Modification	12 Months After Modification	15 Months After Modification
HAMP Fourth Quarter 2011	44,399	4.7%	7.5%	10.7%	13.0%	14.1%
Other Fourth Quarter 2011	72,569	10.3%	17.3%	24.0%	27.7%	27.7%
HAMP First Quarter 2012	37,240	4.9%	8.4%	11.3%	13.0%	13.3%
Other First Quarter 2012	65,861	9.4%	17.5%	23.1%	25.5%	25.5%
HAMP Second Quarter 2012	28,627	4.4%	7.9%	10.1%	11.0%	12.0%
Other Second Quarter 2012	68,088	7.5%	14.5%	17.9%	19.4%	19.4%
HAMP Third Quarter 2012	31,745	4.3%	7.7%	9.4%	11.0%	12.3%
Other Third Quarter 2012	104,764	8.0%	14.6%	17.9%	21.2%	21.2%
HAMP Fourth Quarter 2012	29,314	3.8%	6.2%	8.7%	10.3%	-
Other Fourth Quarter 2012	114,181	8.3%	12.8%	17.5%	20.6%	-
HAMP First Quarter 2013	28,030	3.2%	6.4%	8.9%	-	-
Other First Quarter 2013	110,519	6.5%	13.0%	17.7%	-	-
HAMP Second Quarter 2013	22,613	3.4%	6.9%	-	-	-
Other Second Quarter 2013	85,582	8.3%	15.4%	-	-	-
HAMP Third Quarter 2013	23,159	3.9%	-	-	-	-
Other Third Quarter 2013	76,134	10.6%	-	-	-	-

*Data include all modifications that have had time to age the indicated number of months.

C. Modified Loan Performance, by Change in Monthly Payments

Modifications that reduce borrowers' monthly payments by at least 10 percent consistently show re-default rates lower than those of other modifications—the larger the reduction in monthly payment, the lower the subsequent re-default rates. Lower re-default rates also may result from monthly payments set relative to the borrower's ability to repay, as well as verification of income and completion of a successful trial period.

For servicers and investors, determining the optimal type of modification often requires weighing the reduction in cash flow from loan terms that reduce monthly principal and interest payments, along with the possible costs of delaying foreclosure, against the potential for longer-term sustainability of the payments and ultimate repayment of the mortgage.

Re-Default Rates of Loans by Change in Payment

Tables 35 through 40 present re-default rates, measured as 60 or more days delinquent, for modifications made since January 1, 2008. Data show that re-default rates decrease as reductions in payments increase more than 10 percent. Modification performance has improved over time as modification actions focused on substantively reducing monthly payments and setting payments relative to the borrower's income and ability to pay.

For modifications completed since 2010, actions that resulted in no change to the borrower's monthly payment have performed better than many modifications that reduced payments. Modifications that do not change monthly payment generally freeze the interest rate on an ARM so that rate and payment do not increase. These actions often are offered to borrowers who are current on their payments.

Table 35. Re-Default Rates of Loans Modified in 2008 by Change in Payment (60 or More Days Delinquent)					
	6 Months After Modification	12 Months After Modification	18 Months After Modification	24 Months After Modification	36 Months After Modification
Decreased by 20% or More	26.1%	39.6%	47.0%	49.1%	50.6%
Decreased by 10% to Less Than 20%	32.7%	47.5%	54.3%	55.6%	54.9%
Decreased by Less Than 10%	40.3%	55.2%	60.6%	61.0%	59.0%
Unchanged	53.7%	62.2%	66.3%	67.2%	65.8%
Increased	53.6%	67.3%	71.3%	71.1%	68.3%
Total	44.5%	57.0%	62.0%	62.7%	61.4%

Table 36. Re-Default Rates of Loans Modified in 2009 by Change in Payment (60 or More Days Delinquent)					
	6 Months After Modification	12 Months After Modification	18 Months After Modification	24 Months After Modification	36 Months After Modification
Decreased by 20% or More	19.2%	28.5%	32.8%	34.3%	33.6%
Decreased by 10% to Less Than 20%	29.2%	41.6%	45.0%	45.7%	45.4%
Decreased by Less Than 10%	33.8%	46.7%	49.3%	49.6%	49.9%
Unchanged	48.6%	57.3%	60.8%	61.4%	57.3%
Increased	46.5%	60.0%	62.5%	62.1%	58.6%
Total	32.2%	43.2%	46.5%	47.0%	45.1%

Table 37. Re-Default Rates of Loans Modified in 2010 by Change in Payment
(60 or More Days Delinquent)*

	6 Months After Modification	12 Months After Modification	18 Months After Modification	24 Months After Modification	36 Months After Modification
Decreased by 20% or More	11.4%	17.4%	21.1%	22.3%	21.5%
Decreased by 10% to Less Than 20%	19.8%	30.3%	35.6%	37.3%	37.0%
Decreased by Less Than 10%	26.1%	37.4%	42.7%	43.9%	42.8%
Unchanged	18.8%	23.0%	24.8%	24.1%	20.6%
Increased	32.8%	44.1%	48.1%	48.8%	45.0%
Total	17.3%	25.4%	29.5%	30.6%	29.2%

Table 38. Re-Default Rates of Loans Modified in 2011 by Change in Payment
(60 or More Days Delinquent)*

	6 Months After Modification	12 Months After Modification	18 Months After Modification	24 Months After Modification	36 Months After Modification
Decreased by 20% or More	11.4%	17.4%	21.1%	22.3%	-
Decreased by 10% to Less Than 20%	19.8%	30.3%	35.6%	37.3%	-
Decreased by Less Than 10%	26.1%	37.4%	42.7%	43.9%	-
Unchanged	18.8%	23.0%	24.8%	24.1%	-
Increased	32.8%	44.1%	48.1%	48.8%	-
Total	17.3%	25.4%	29.5%	30.6%	-

Table 39. Re-Default Rates of Loans Modified in 2012 by Change in Payment
(60 or More Days Delinquent)*

	6 Months After Modification	12 Months After Modification	18 Months After Modification	24 Months after Modification	36 Months After Modification
Decreased by 20% or More	8.8%	13.2%	15.5%	-	-
Decreased by 10% to Less Than 20%	12.5%	19.5%	22.2%	-	-
Decreased by Less Than 10%	22.1%	33.3%	36.1%	-	-
Unchanged	9.9%	11.3%	14.3%	-	-
Increased	29.0%	38.8%	41.9%	-	-
Total	12.7%	18.8%	21.1%	-	-

Table 40. Re-Default Rates of Loans Modified in 2013 by Change in Payment
(60 or More Days Delinquent)*

	6 Months After Modification	12 Months After Modification	18 Months After Modification	24 Months after Modification	36 Months After Modification
Decreased by 20% or More	8.6%	-	-	-	-
Decreased by 10% to Less Than 20%	13.6%	-	-	-	-
Decreased by Less Than 10%	21.3%	-	-	-	-
Unchanged	19.6%	-	-	-	-
Increased	24.6%	-	-	-	-
Total	12.5%	-	-	-	-

*Data in tables 37-40 include modifications that were originated that year and aged the indicated number of months.

60+ Delinquency at Six Months After Modification by Change in Monthly Payment

Modifications that reduced monthly principal and interest payments by at least 10 percent consistently performed better than other modifications. Modifications with the greatest decrease in monthly payments consistently had the lowest re-default rates. Modifications that resulted in no change to the borrowers' monthly payments generally have performed better than many modifications that reduced payments because these modifications tend to be offered to borrowers with ARMs who have not defaulted on their payments.

Table 41. 60+ Delinquency at Six Months After Modification by Change in Monthly Payment						
	Decreased by 20% or More	Decreased by 10% to Less Than 20%	Decreased by Less Than 10%	Unchanged	Increased	Overall
Second Quarter 2012	9.1%	11.3%	22.3%	7.9%	30.9%	12.5%
Third Quarter 2012	8.7%	12.6%	23.3%	7.3%	30.8%	13.0%
Fourth Quarter 2012	8.0%	11.9%	20.1%	20.5%	23.6%	11.4%
First Quarter 2013	8.2%	12.1%	19.8%	21.0%	22.5%	11.6%
Second Quarter 2013	9.2%	15.8%	23.5%	18.1%	27.1%	13.6%
Total for the quarters above	8.5%	12.6%	21.7%	10.0%	26.9%	12.3%

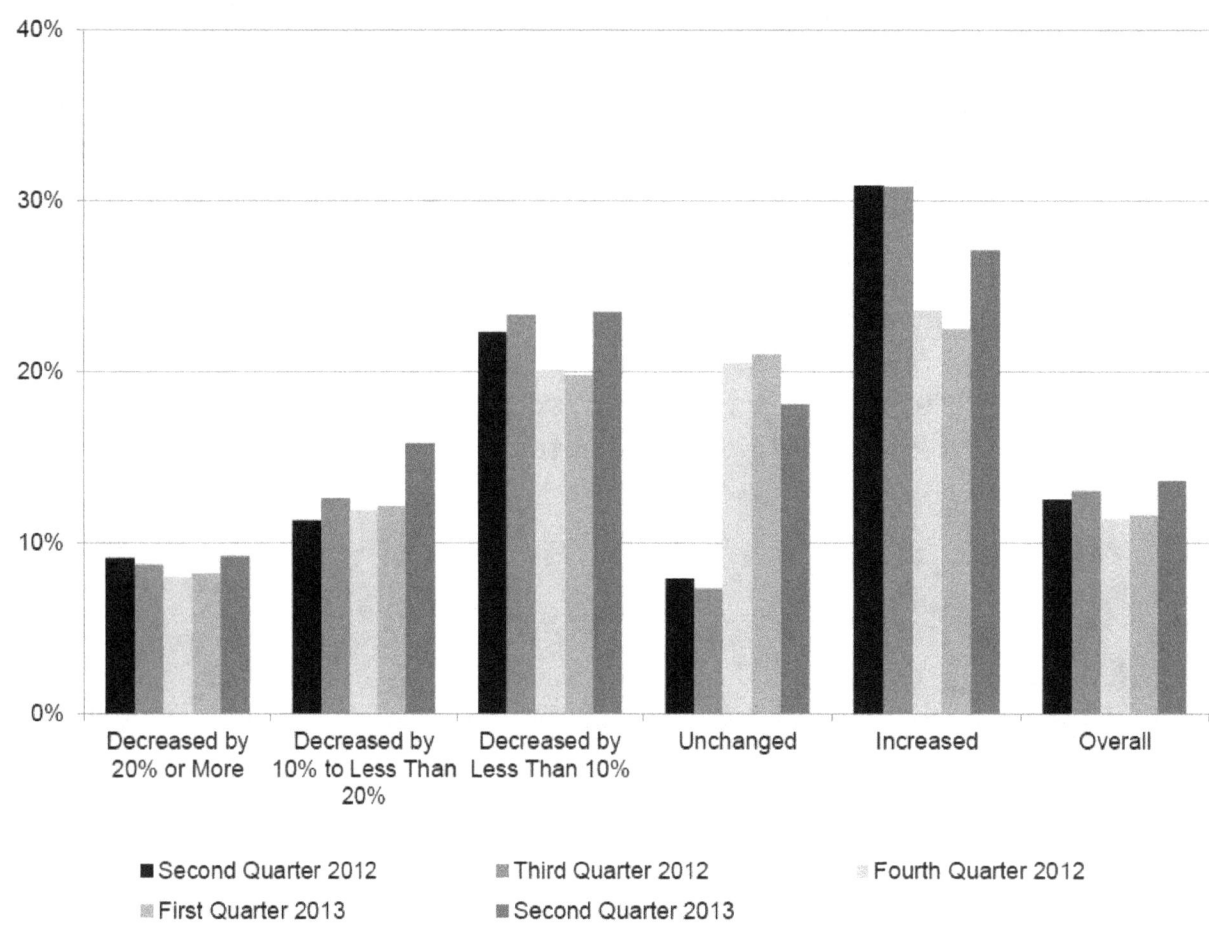

Figure 14. 60+ Delinquency at Six Months After Modification by Change in Monthly Payment

Status of Mortgages Modified in 2008–3Q 2013

Servicers implemented 3,388,010 modifications from January 1, 2008, through September 30, 2013. Of these modifications, 40.3 percent were current and performing at the end of the fourth quarter of 2013 with another 3.1 percent paid off. Almost 17 percent of these modifications were delinquent, while 12.3 percent were in the process of foreclosure or had completed the foreclosure process. HAMP modifications implemented since the third quarter of 2009 have performed better than other modifications. Modifications that reduced borrowers' monthly payments by 10 percent or more performed significantly better than other modifications. Of the 2,163,438 modifications that reduced payments by 10 percent or more, 48.4 percent were current or paid off at the end of 2013, compared with 34.6 percent of modifications that reduced payments by less than 10 percent.

	Total	Current	30–59 Days Delinquent	Seriously Delinquent	Foreclosures in Process	Completed Foreclosures	Paid Off	No Longer in the Portfolio*
Table 42. Status of Mortgages Modified in 2008–3Q 2013								
2008	443,294	19.0%	3.8%	8.2%	4.0%	17.0%	4.7%	43.2%
2009	593,884	28.4%	4.8%	10.5%	4.8%	13.2%	4.5%	33.8%
2010	955,422	37.6%	5.5%	10.5%	4.8%	8.8%	3.5%	29.3%
2011	569,553	44.7%	6.2%	11.8%	4.9%	4.5%	2.7%	25.2%
2012	479,820	56.7%	7.3%	12.3%	4.2%	1.2%	1.6%	16.7%
2013	346,037	65.6%	8.9%	11.0%	2.1%	0.2%	0.6%	11.5%
Total	3,388,010	40.3%	5.9%	10.7%	4.3%	8.0%	3.1%	27.6%
HAMP Modification Performance Compared With Other Modifications**								
Other Modifications	1,845,827	43.9%	7.0%	13.3%	5.0%	6.6%	3.1%	21.1%
HAMP Modifications	761,043	51.0%	4.9%	6.5%	2.9%	3.6%	1.9%	29.2%
Modifications That Reduced Payments by 10 Percent or More								
	2,163,438	46.1%	5.9%	9.3%	3.6%	5.4%	2.3%	27.3%
Modifications That Reduced Payments by Less Than 10 Percent								
	1,224,572	30.0%	5.8%	13.3%	5.6%	12.5%	4.6%	28.2%

*Processing constraints prevented some servicers from reporting the reason for removal from the portfolio.

**Modifications used to compare with HAMP modifications only include modifications implemented from the third quarter of 2009 through the third quarter of 2013.

Part III: Home Forfeiture Actions—Foreclosures, Short Sales, and Deed-in-Lieu-of-Foreclosure Actions

Completed Foreclosures and Other Home Forfeiture Actions

Home forfeiture actions—foreclosure sales, short sales, and deed-in-lieu-of-foreclosure actions—totaled 84,031 during the fourth quarter of 2013, a decrease of 50.3 percent from a year earlier. The number of completed foreclosures decreased to 60,765—down 26.6 percent from the previous quarter and 42.6 percent from a year earlier. Short sales decreased 32.3 percent from the previous quarter and 65.8 percent from a year earlier. Short sales were 25.2 percent of total home forfeiture actions, down from 36.5 percent a year earlier. Deed-in-lieu-of-foreclosure actions remained a small portion of home forfeiture actions during the quarter.

Table 43. Completed Foreclosures and Other Home Forfeiture Actions							
	12/31/12	3/31/13	6/30/13	9/30/13	12/31/13	1Q %Change	1Y %Change
Completed Foreclosures	105,875	84,977	79,960	82,841	60,765	-26.6%	-42.6%
New Short Sales	61,761	43,143	39,207	31,261	21,149	-32.3%	-65.8%
New Deed-in-Lieu-of-Foreclosure Actions	1,428	3,596	2,579	2,112	2,117	0.2%	48.2%
Total	169,064	131,716	121,746	116,214	84,031	-27.7%	-50.3%

Newly Initiated Foreclosures

Servicers initiate foreclosure actions at defined stages of loan delinquency. Foreclosure actions progress to sale of the property only if servicers and borrowers cannot arrange a permanent loss mitigation action, modification, or alternate workout solution or home sale. Newly initiated foreclosures decreased to 124,468 in the fourth quarter of 2013, a decrease of 4.7 percent from the previous quarter and 20.6 percent from a year earlier.

Table 44. Number of Newly Initiated Foreclosures							
	12/31/12	3/31/13	6/30/13	9/30/13	12/31/13	1Q %Change	1Y %Change
Prime	63,834	72,198	61,405	52,211	49,420	-5.3%	-22.6%
Alt-A	32,812	38,052	32,749	29,287	27,910	-4.7%	-14.9%
Subprime	32,886	38,464	32,667	28,491	27,820	-2.4%	-15.4%
Other	27,241	29,646	23,771	20,603	19,318	-6.2%	-29.1%
Total	156,773	178,360	150,592	130,592	124,468	-4.7%	-20.6%

Figure 15. Number of Newly Initiated Foreclosures

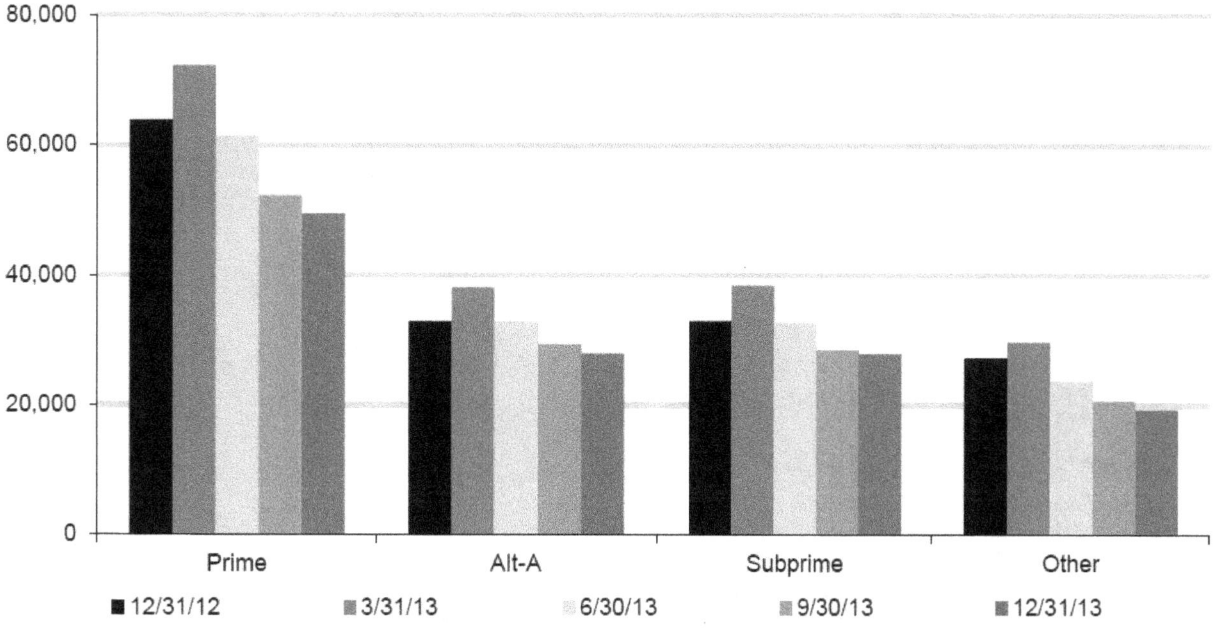

Foreclosures in Process

The number of mortgages in the process of foreclosure decreased to 523,528 at the end of 2013, down 13.4 percent from the previous quarter and 45.9 percent from a year earlier. The percentage of mortgages in the portfolio that were in some stage of the foreclosure process at the end of 2013 was 2.1 percent, a decrease of 10.9 percent from the previous quarter and 37.0 percent from a year earlier.

Table 45. Foreclosures in Process							
Percentage of Foreclosures in Process Relative to Mortgages in That Risk Category							
	12/31/12	3/31/13	6/30/13	9/30/13	12/31/13	1Q %Change	1Y %Change
Prime	2.0%	1.9%	1.6%	1.3%	1.2%	-11.5%	-40.8%
Alt-A	6.1%	6.0%	5.3%	4.6%	4.2%	-8.9%	-30.1%
Subprime	10.7%	10.5%	9.3%	8.0%	7.3%	-8.4%	-31.9%
Other	4.9%	5.0%	4.6%	4.0%	3.7%	-7.8%	-25.0%
Total	3.3%	3.2%	2.8%	2.4%	2.1%	-10.9%	-37.0%
Number of Foreclosures in Process							
Prime	422,472	390,415	316,235	255,583	221,675	-13.3%	-47.5%
Alt-A	188,577	179,261	148,632	122,232	107,033	-12.4%	-43.2%
Subprime	213,843	200,731	162,774	130,037	111,260	-14.4%	-48.0%
Other	142,575	136,821	116,728	96,911	83,560	-13.8%	-41.4%
Total	967,467	907,228	744,369	604,763	523,528	-13.4%	-45.9%

Figure 16. Number of Foreclosures in Process

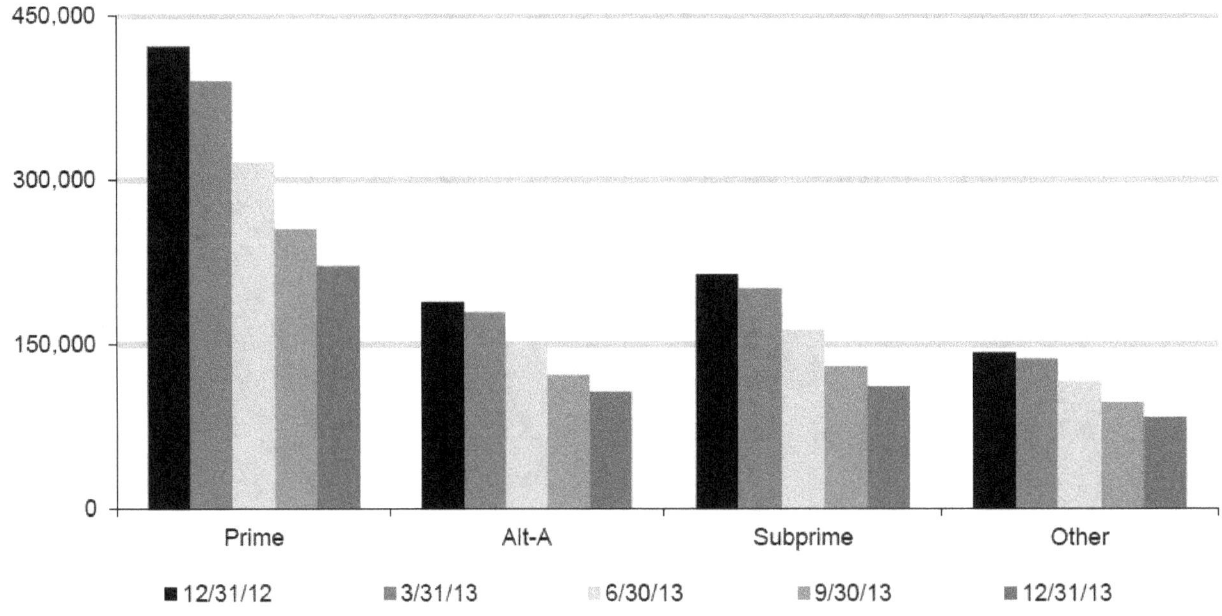

Completed Foreclosures

The number of completed foreclosures was 60,765 during the quarter—a decrease of 26.6 percent from the previous quarter and 42.6 percent from a year earlier. The percentage of mortgages that completed the foreclosure process during the fourth quarter of 2013 was 0.2 percent of all mortgages serviced, a decrease of 24.5 percent from the previous quarter and 33.2 percent from a year earlier.

Table 46. Completed Foreclosures							
Percentage of Completed Foreclosures Relative to Mortgages in That Risk Category							
	12/31/12	3/31/13	6/30/13	9/30/13	12/31/13	1Q %Change	1Y %Change
Prime	0.2%	0.2%	0.2%	0.2%	0.1%	-23.8%	-38.9%
Alt-A	0.7%	0.5%	0.6%	0.6%	0.5%	-24.3%	-26.4%
Subprime	1.1%	0.9%	1.0%	1.1%	0.8%	-23.2%	-25.2%
Other	0.6%	0.5%	0.5%	0.6%	0.5%	-21.9%	-17.9%
Total	0.4%	0.3%	0.3%	0.3%	0.2%	-24.5%	-33.2%
Number of Completed Foreclosures							
Prime	46,647	39,255	34,686	33,817	25,253	-25.3%	-45.9%
Alt-A	20,764	16,005	15,943	17,062	12,410	-27.3%	-40.2%
Subprime	22,562	16,588	16,654	17,992	12,902	-28.3%	-42.8%
Other	15,902	13,129	12,677	13,970	10,200	-27.0%	-35.9%
Total	105,875	84,977	79,960	82,841	60,765	-26.6%	-42.6%

Figure 17. Number of Completed Foreclosures

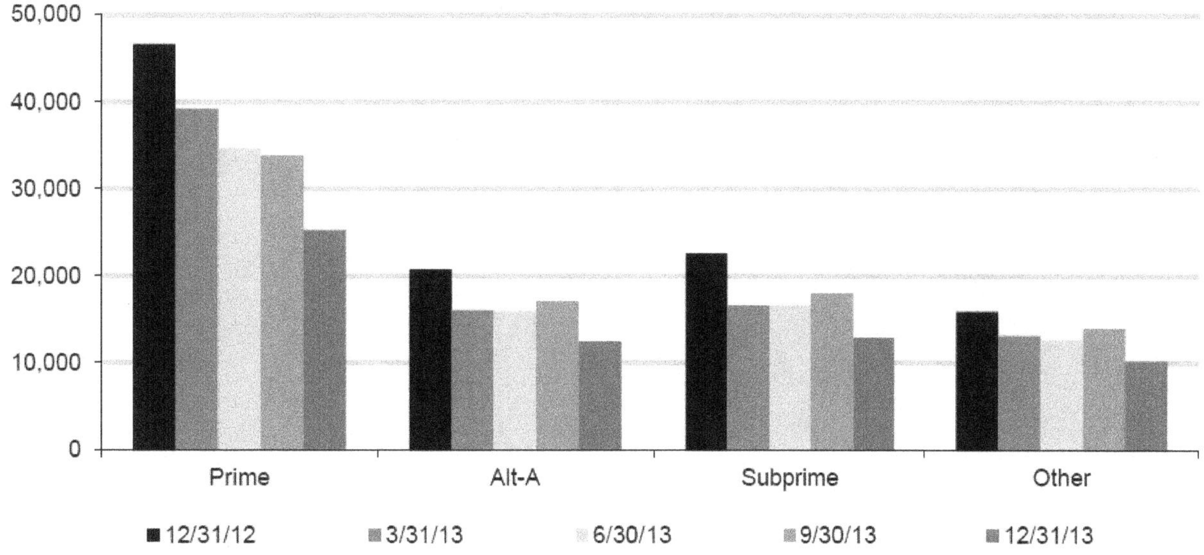

Completed Short Sales and Deeds in Lieu of Foreclosure

The number of completed short sales and deeds in lieu of foreclosure decreased to 23,266 during the quarter—down 30.3 percent from the previous quarter and 63.2 percent from a year earlier. Short sales and deeds in lieu of foreclosure as a percentage of all mortgages serviced at the end of 2013 were 0.1 percent, down 28.2 percent from the previous quarter and 57.2 percent from a year earlier.

Table 47. Completed Short Sales and Deeds in Lieu of Foreclosure							
Percentage of Completed Foreclosures Relative to Mortgages in That Risk Category							
	12/31/12	3/31/13	6/30/13	9/30/13	12/31/13	1Q %Change	1Y %Change
Prime	0.2%	0.1%	0.1%	0.1%	0.1%	-29.6%	-60.6%
Alt-A	0.3%	0.2%	0.2%	0.2%	0.2%	-25.7%	-50.3%
Subprime	0.4%	0.3%	0.3%	0.3%	0.2%	-26.4%	-50.8%
Other	0.2%	0.1%	0.2%	0.1%	0.1%	-22.7%	-44.9%
Total	0.2%	0.2%	0.2%	0.1%	0.1%	-28.2%	-57.2%
Number of Completed Foreclosures							
Prime	39,498	28,731	25,236	19,959	13,781	-31.0%	-65.1%
Alt-A	9,513	7,418	6,699	5,382	3,844	-28.6%	-59.6%
Subprime	8,519	6,494	5,762	4,658	3,203	-31.2%	-62.4%
Other	5,659	4,096	4,089	3,374	2,438	-27.7%	-56.9%
Overall	63,189	46,739	41,786	33,373	23,266	-30.3%	-63.2%

Figure 18. Number of Completed Short Sales and Deeds in Lieu of Foreclosure

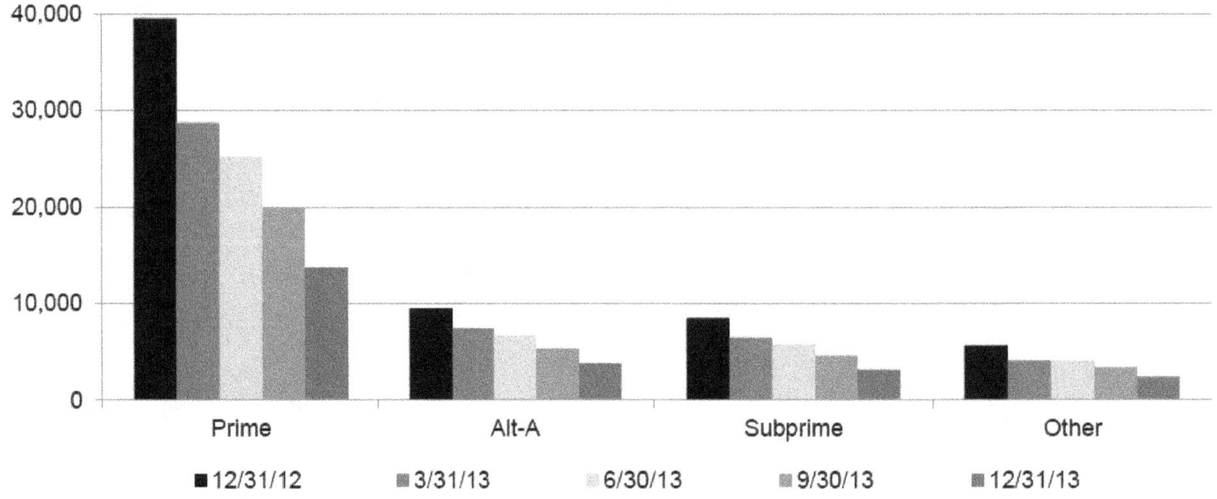

New Home Retention Actions Relative to Forfeiture Actions, by Risk Category

New home retention actions continued to exceed completed home forfeitures as servicers initiated almost three times as many home retention actions as home forfeiture actions during the quarter. The percentage of new home retention actions relative to home forfeitures continued to be highest for Alt-A and subprime loans and lowest for prime and other loans during the fourth quarter of 2013.

Table 48. Percentage of New Home Retention Actions Relative to Forfeiture Actions, by Risk Category							
	12/31/12	3/31/13	6/30/13	9/30/13	12/31/13	1Q %Change	1Y %Change
Prime	188.9%	229.3%	228.2%	239.6%	252.9%	5.6%	33.9%
Alt-A	262.7%	321.9%	313.3%	329.9%	359.9%	9.1%	37.0%
Subprime	271.9%	340.3%	309.8%	304.8%	328.4%	7.7%	20.8%
Other	189.7%	229.1%	232.3%	236.8%	258.8%	9.3%	36.4%
Overall	217.5%	265.2%	259.6%	269.4%	289.0%	7.3%	32.9%

Figure 19. Percentage of New Home Retention Actions Relative to Forfeiture Actions, by Risk Category

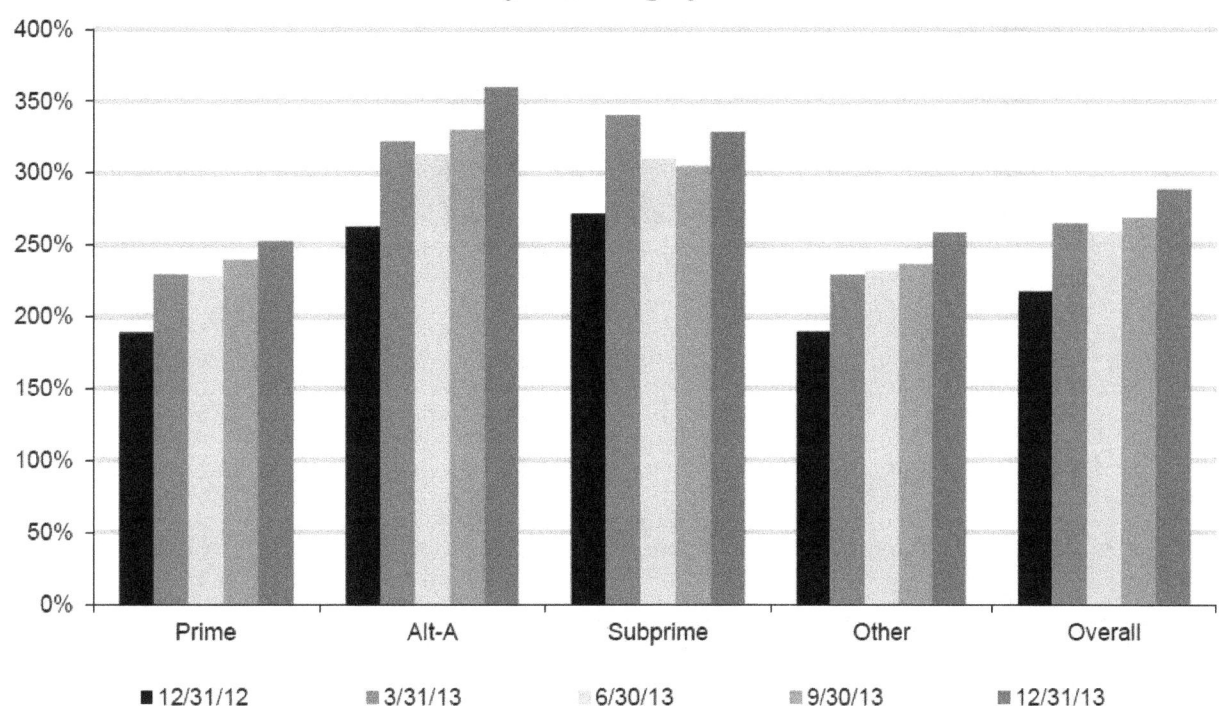

Appendixes

Appendix A—New Loan Modifications

There were 72,466 loan modifications completed during the fourth quarter of 2013—a decrease of 27.0 percent from the previous quarter and 49.5 percent from a year earlier.

Table 49. Number of New Loan Modifications							
	12/31/12	3/31/13	6/30/13	9/30/13	12/31/13	1Q %Change	1Y %Change
Prime	63,211	62,195	45,277	41,831	30,690	-26.6%	-51.4%
Alt-A	30,708	29,415	24,070	21,758	16,244	-25.3%	-47.1%
Subprime	35,091	32,730	26,393	23,398	16,295	-30.4%	-53.6%
Other	14,485	14,209	12,455	12,306	9,237	-24.9%	-36.2%
Total	143,495	138,549	108,195	99,293	72,466	-27.0%	-49.5%

Figure 20. Number of New Loan Modifications

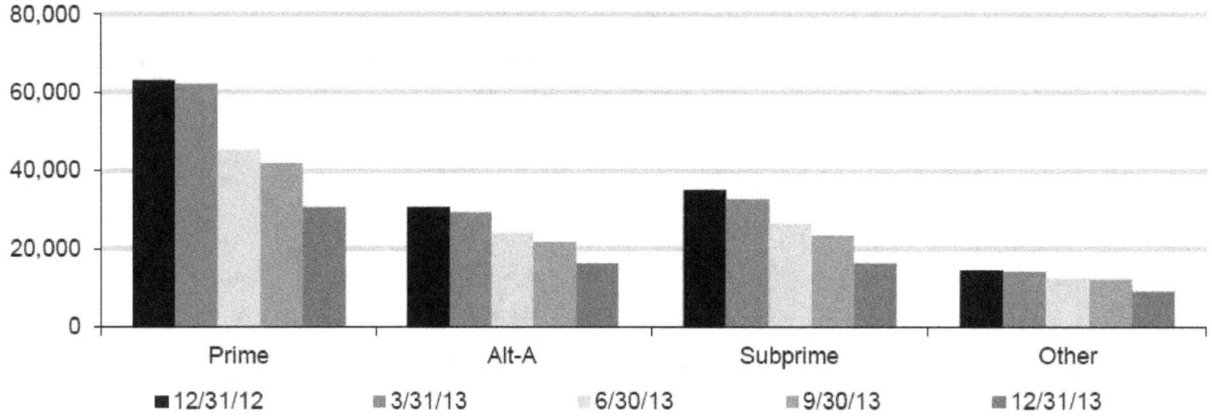

Appendix B—New Trial-Period Plans

Servicers initiated 82,269 trial-period plans during the fourth quarter of 2013, a decrease of 18.7 percent from the previous quarter and 32.4 percent from a year earlier.

Table 50. Number of New Trial-Period Plans						
	12/31/12	3/31/13	6/30/13	9/30/13	12/31/13	1Q %Change	1Y %Change
Prime	61,603	54,191	49,651	44,992	35,846	-20.3%	-41.8%
Alt-A	26,355	22,248	22,289	24,569	20,350	-17.2%	-22.8%
Subprime	24,367	19,413	19,021	21,202	17,499	-17.5%	-28.2%
Other	9,405	7,809	9,532	10,399	8,574	-17.5%	-8.8%
Total	121,730	103,661	100,493	101,162	82,269	-18.7%	-32.4%

Figure 21. Number of New Trial-Period Plans

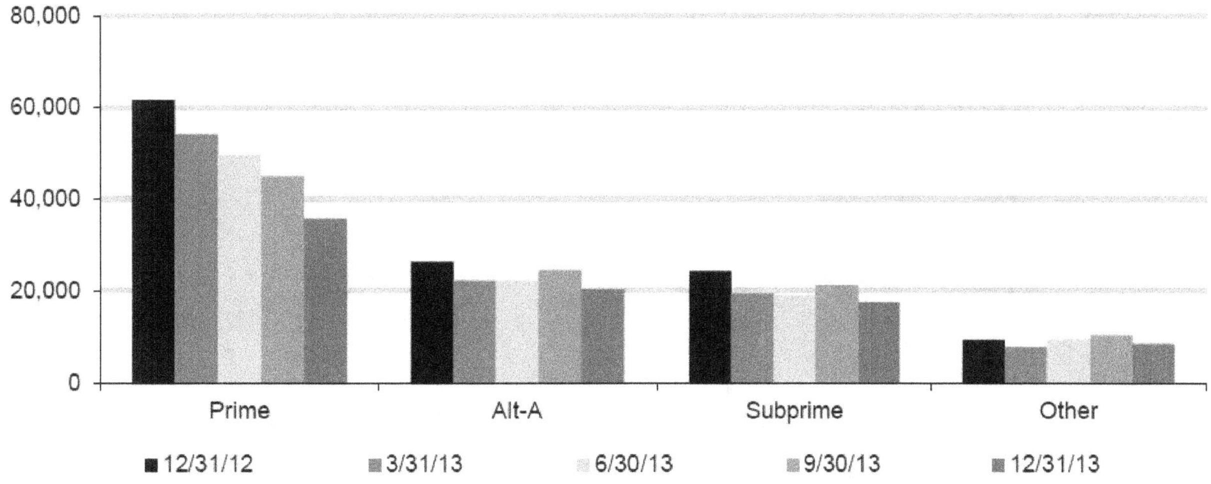

Appendix C—New Payment Plans

New payment plans fell to 88,093 during the fourth quarter of 2013, a decrease of 21.7 percent from the previous quarter.

Table 51. Number of New Payment Plans							
	12/31/12	3/31/13	6/30/13	9/30/13	12/31/13	1Q %Change	1Y %Change
Prime	37,922	39,529	41,831	42,039	32,195	-23.4%	-15.1%
Alt-A	22,482	23,725	24,587	27,712	21,908	-20.9%	-2.6%
Subprime	25,040	26,409	24,023	24,448	19,100	-21.9%	-23.7%
Other	17,002	17,450	16,962	18,369	14,890	-18.9%	-12.4%
Total	102,446	107,113	107,403	112,568	88,093	-21.7%	-14.0%

Figure 22. Number of New Payment Plans

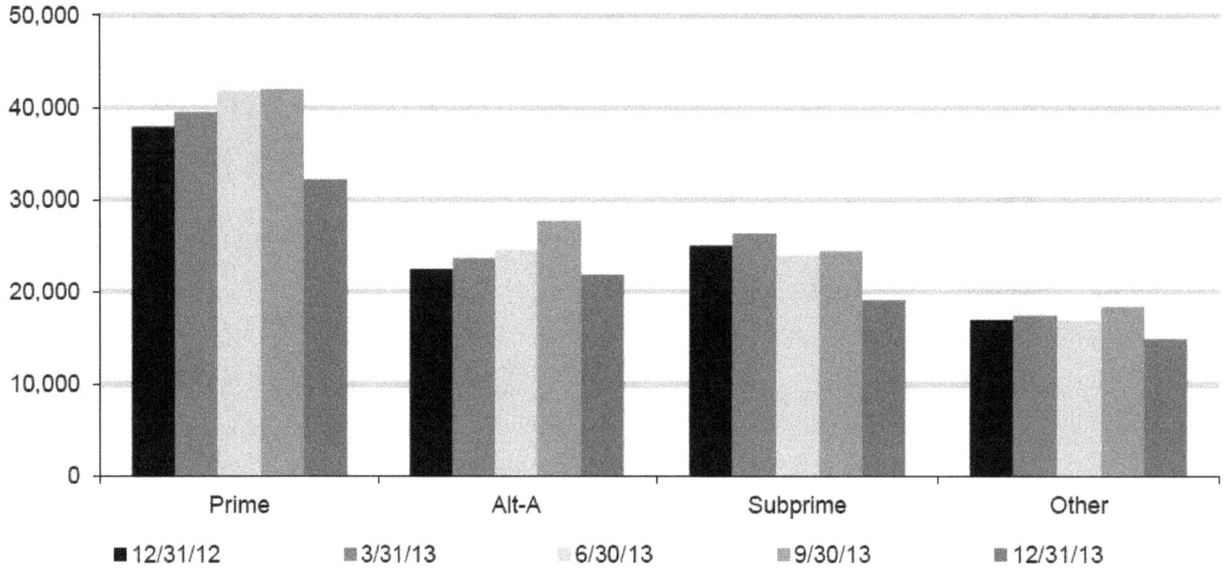

Appendix D—Breakdown of Individual and Combination Modification Actions

Servicers generally use a combination of actions to reduce monthly payments and achieve payment sustainability when modifying a mortgage. Servicers changed more than one loan term in 95.3 percent of all modifications completed during the fourth quarter of 2013.

Table 52. Changes in Terms for Modifications Made Through the Fourth Quarter of 2013							
(Percentage of Modifications in Each Category)							
	12/31/12	3/31/13	6/30/13	9/30/13	12/31/13	1Q %Change	1Y %Change
Combination*	89.9%	85.8%	89.7%	92.3%	95.3%	3.3%	6.1%
Capitalization	1.4%	1.7%	1.8%	2.1%	2.4%	13.7%	80.0%
Rate Reduction	6.5%	11.1%	5.6%	2.5%	0.7%	-70.9%	-88.8%
Rate Freeze	0.1%	0.0%	0.0%	0.0%	0.0%	14.2%	-88.1%
Term Extension	0.9%	0.6%	1.2%	0.6%	0.6%	-7.1%	-30.7%
Principal Reduction	0.1%	0.1%	0.1%	0.0%	0.0%	105.5%	-91.1%
Principal Deferral	0.1%	0.1%	0.1%	0.2%	0.2%	-24.8%	39.9%
Not Reported**	1.1%	0.6%	1.4%	2.2%	0.7%	-68.1%	-37.8%
(Number of Changes in Each Category)							
Combination*	128,974	118,853	97,053	91,658	69,096	-24.6%	-46.4%
Capitalization	1,944	2,354	1,997	2,129	1,767	-17.0%	-9.1%
Rate Reduction	9,271	15,349	6,104	2,462	523	-78.8%	-94.4%
Rate Freeze	83	12	2	6	5	-16.7%	-94.0%
Term Extension	1,240	868	1,312	640	434	-32.2%	-65.0%
Principal Reduction	200	103	88	6	9	50.0%	-95.5%
Principal Deferral	184	110	143	237	130	-45.1%	-29.3%
Not Reported***	1,599	900	1,496	2,155	502	-76.7%	-68.6%
All Modifications	143,495	138,549	108,195	99,293	72,466	-27.0%	-49.5%

*Combination modifications result in a change to two or more loan terms. All other modification types detailed in this table involve only the individual listed action.

**Comparison to previous year value is not meaningful.

***Processing constraints at some servicers prevented them from reporting specific modified term(s).

Changes in Terms for Combination Modification Actions

Of the 69,096 modifications completed during the fourth quarter of 2013 that changed more than one term of the mortgage contract, 88.9 percent included capitalization of missed fees and payments, 79.6 percent included interest-rate reduction, and 79.0 percent included an extension of the loan maturity. Principal deferral was included in 31.9 percent of the combination modifications implemented during the quarter, and principal reduction was included in 11.0 percent. Because combination modifications changed more than one term, the sum of the individual actions exceeded 100 percent of total combination modifications.

Table 53. Changes in Terms for Combination Modifications Through the Fourth Quarter of 2013

(Percentage of Modifications in Each Category)							
	12/31/12	3/31/13	6/30/13	9/30/13	12/31/13	1Q %Change	1Y %Change
Capitalization	92.7%	90.5%	89.0%	88.2%	88.9%	0.7%	-4.1%
Rate Reduction	74.3%	80.4%	84.0%	82.8%	79.6%	-3.8%	7.2%
Rate Freeze	4.3%	4.3%	5.8%	5.9%	7.3%	24.3%	70.1%
Term Extension	64.6%	69.6%	74.1%	74.4%	79.0%	6.2%	22.4%
Principal Reduction	22.1%	17.6%	13.5%	14.7%	11.0%	-25.1%	-50.2%
Principal Deferral	22.7%	21.2%	22.7%	27.2%	31.9%	17.5%	40.8%
(Total Number of Changes in Each Category)							
Capitalization	119,510	107,528	86,421	80,869	61,402	-24.1%	-48.6%
Rate Reduction	95,844	95,561	81,535	75,847	55,031	-27.4%	-42.6%
Rate Freeze	5,561	5,109	5,617	5,407	5,067	-6.3%	-8.9%
Term Extension	83,278	82,726	71,942	68,180	54,592	-19.9%	-34.4%
Principal Reduction	28,565	20,930	13,062	13,496	7,625	-43.5%	-73.3%
Principal Deferral	29,261	25,162	22,052	24,913	22,065	-11.4%	-24.6%

Appendix E—Mortgage Modification Data by State

The following tables present certain mortgage modification data by state, the District of Columbia, and U.S. territories (the latter are included in the category labeled "Other"). These data fulfill reporting requirements in the Dodd–Frank Wall Street Reform and Consumer Protection Act of 2010 (Public Law 111-203).

Table 54 presents the number and percentage of HAMP modifications and other modifications in each state during the fourth quarter of 2013. Tables 55 and 56 present the number and percentage of each type of action included in modifications made during the quarter in each state, the District of Columbia, and U.S. territories. Tables 57 and 58 present the number and percentage of each type of action included in combination modifications made during the quarter in each state, the District of Columbia, and U.S. territories. Tables 59 and 60 present the number and percentage of modifications made during the quarter in each state, the District of Columbia, and U.S. territories by the amount of change in the borrowers' monthly principal and interest payments. Tables 61 and 62 present the number and percentage of modifications made in the second quarter of 2013 that were 60 or more days delinquent or in the process of foreclosure at the end of 2013.

Table 54. Number and Percentage of Mortgage Modifications Implemented in the Fourth Quarter of 2013					
	HAMP Modifications		Other Modifications		Total Modifications	
States	Total	% of State Total	Total	% of State Total	Total	% of Total
Total - All States	20,829	28.7%	51,637	71.3%	72,466	100.0%
Alabama	219	25.3%	646	74.7%	865	1.2%
Alaska	12	27.9%	31	72.1%	43	0.1%
Arizona	356	29.2%	863	70.8%	1,219	1.7%
Arkansas	89	25.5%	260	74.5%	349	0.5%
California	3,738	36.4%	6,526	63.6%	10,264	14.2%
Colorado	277	32.1%	586	67.9%	863	1.2%
Connecticut	327	28.1%	837	71.9%	1,164	1.6%
Delaware	94	22.8%	318	77.2%	412	0.6%
District of Columbia	32	21.5%	117	78.5%	149	0.2%
Florida	2,355	29.6%	5,610	70.4%	7,965	11.0%
Georgia	833	26.1%	2,361	73.9%	3,194	4.4%
Hawaii	32	18.8%	138	81.2%	170	0.2%
Idaho	59	19.7%	241	80.3%	300	0.4%
Illinois	1,198	29.0%	2,930	71.0%	4,128	5.7%
Indiana	362	27.9%	934	72.1%	1,296	1.8%
Iowa	84	23.0%	282	77.0%	366	0.5%
Kansas	64	23.1%	213	76.9%	277	0.4%
Kentucky	122	22.8%	414	77.2%	536	0.7%
Louisiana	147	20.5%	571	79.5%	718	1.0%
Maine	56	22.4%	194	77.6%	250	0.3%
Maryland	720	27.9%	1,863	72.1%	2,583	3.6%
Massachusetts	421	29.2%	1,022	70.8%	1,443	2.0%
Michigan	386	23.1%	1,285	76.9%	1,671	2.3%
Minnesota	332	30.4%	761	69.6%	1,093	1.5%
Mississippi	96	24.9%	289	75.1%	385	0.5%
Missouri	332	31.6%	719	68.4%	1,051	1.5%
Montana	27	25.2%	80	74.8%	107	0.1%
Nebraska	57	28.9%	140	71.1%	197	0.3%
Nevada	323	28.6%	808	71.4%	1,131	1.6%
New Hampshire	77	27.1%	207	72.9%	284	0.4%
New Jersey	963	27.7%	2,519	72.3%	3,482	4.8%
New Mexico	84	22.0%	297	78.0%	381	0.5%
New York	1,320	30.6%	2,993	69.4%	4,313	6.0%
North Carolina	627	25.5%	1,832	74.5%	2,459	3.4%
North Dakota	4	15.4%	22	84.6%	26	0.0%
Ohio	626	28.9%	1,543	71.1%	2,169	3.0%
Oklahoma	80	21.2%	297	78.8%	377	0.5%
Oregon	190	24.5%	585	75.5%	775	1.1%
Pennsylvania	681	26.6%	1,881	73.4%	2,562	3.5%
Rhode Island	80	27.5%	211	72.5%	291	0.4%
South Carolina	221	20.7%	845	79.3%	1,066	1.5%
South Dakota	10	20.4%	39	79.6%	49	0.1%
Tennessee	269	26.8%	734	73.2%	1,003	1.4%
Texas	1,062	28.1%	2,713	71.9%	3,775	5.2%
Utah	148	29.0%	362	71.0%	510	0.7%
Vermont	13	11.9%	96	88.1%	109	0.2%
Virginia	477	27.9%	1,232	72.1%	1,709	2.4%
Washington	434	25.6%	1,264	74.4%	1,698	2.3%
West Virginia	25	14.3%	150	85.7%	175	0.2%
Wisconsin	232	26.4%	648	73.6%	880	1.2%
Wyoming	8	16.7%	40	83.3%	48	0.1%
Other	48	35.3%	88	64.7%	136	0.2%

Table 55. Number of Mortgage Modification Actions
Implemented in the Fourth Quarter of 2013

States	Capitalization	Rate Reduction or Freeze	Term Extension	Principal Reductions	Principal Deferral	Combination	Not Reported	Total Modifications
Total - All States	1,767	528	434	9	130	69,096	502	72,466
Alabama	27	1	2	0	0	832	3	865
Alaska	0	0	0	0	0	43	0	43
Arizona	30	9	10	1	2	1,161	6	1,219
Arkansas	8	2	2	0	0	336	1	349
California	274	129	48	2	47	9,691	73	10,264
Colorado	36	7	8	0	1	807	4	863
Connecticut	32	8	8	0	3	1,103	10	1,164
Delaware	4	1	2	0	0	405	0	412
District of Columbia	13	2	0	0	1	132	1	149
Florida	160	62	29	1	14	7,660	39	7,965
Georgia	82	31	20	0	3	3,042	16	3,194
Hawaii	6	3	5	0	0	156	0	170
Idaho	10	1	3	0	0	285	1	300
Illinois	54	22	32	2	4	3,999	15	4,128
Indiana	32	8	10	0	0	1,236	10	1,296
Iowa	11	1	3	0	0	350	1	366
Kansas	8	1	3	0	0	265	0	277
Kentucky	18	4	5	0	0	508	1	536
Louisiana	19	2	4	0	0	691	2	718
Maine	7	1	2	0	0	237	3	250
Maryland	87	19	26	0	11	2,421	19	2,583
Massachusetts	43	9	10	0	2	1,366	13	1,443
Michigan	35	8	9	1	3	1,602	13	1,671
Minnesota	18	7	2	0	3	1,063	0	1,093
Mississippi	14	2	2	0	0	363	4	385
Missouri	27	9	4	0	1	1,008	2	1,051
Montana	4	1	0	0	0	101	1	107
Nebraska	6	0	0	0	0	190	1	197
Nevada	22	9	9	1	1	1,083	6	1,131
New Hampshire	8	0	1	0	0	269	6	284
New Jersey	57	18	24	1	3	3,356	23	3,482
New Mexico	6	1	1	0	1	370	2	381
New York	65	27	22	0	13	4,069	117	4,313
North Carolina	71	10	23	0	2	2,343	10	2,459
North Dakota	0	0	0	0	0	26	0	26
Ohio	50	10	5	0	0	2,093	11	2,169
Oklahoma	6	4	0	0	0	367	0	377
Oregon	15	4	1	0	3	745	7	775
Pennsylvania	61	9	18	0	1	2,447	26	2,562
Rhode Island	9	1	3	0	0	276	2	291
South Carolina	44	9	5	0	0	1,004	4	1,066
South Dakota	2	0	0	0	0	47	0	49
Tennessee	29	5	7	0	1	958	3	1,003
Texas	117	38	28	0	2	3,575	15	3,775
Utah	18	0	2	0	0	487	3	510
Vermont	2	1	0	0	0	106	0	109
Virginia	53	14	14	0	3	1,609	16	1,709
Washington	35	12	16	0	5	1,620	10	1,698
West Virginia	11	2	2	0	0	158	2	175
Wisconsin	19	4	4	0	0	853	0	880
Wyoming	1	0	0	0	0	47	0	48
Other	1	0	0	0	0	135	0	136

Table 56. Percentage of Mortgage Modification Actions Implemented in the Fourth Quarter of 2013							
States	Capitalization	Rate Reduction or Freeze	Term Extension	Principal Reduction	Principal Deferral	Combination	Not Reported	Total Modifications
Total - All States	2.4%	0.7%	0.6%	0.0%	0.2%	95.3%	0.7%	72,466
Alabama	3.1%	0.1%	0.2%	0.0%	0.0%	96.2%	0.3%	865
Alaska	0.0%	0.0%	0.0%	0.0%	0.0%	100.0%	0.0%	43
Arizona	2.5%	0.7%	0.8%	0.1%	0.2%	95.2%	0.5%	1,219
Arkansas	2.3%	0.6%	0.6%	0.0%	0.0%	96.3%	0.3%	349
California	2.7%	1.3%	0.5%	0.0%	0.5%	94.4%	0.7%	10,264
Colorado	4.2%	0.8%	0.9%	0.0%	0.1%	93.5%	0.5%	863
Connecticut	2.7%	0.7%	0.7%	0.0%	0.3%	94.8%	0.9%	1,164
Delaware	1.0%	0.2%	0.5%	0.0%	0.0%	98.3%	0.0%	412
District of Columbia	8.7%	1.3%	0.0%	0.0%	0.7%	88.6%	0.7%	149
Florida	2.0%	0.8%	0.4%	0.0%	0.2%	96.2%	0.5%	7,965
Georgia	2.6%	1.0%	0.6%	0.0%	0.1%	95.2%	0.5%	3,194
Hawaii	3.5%	1.8%	2.9%	0.0%	0.0%	91.8%	0.0%	170
Idaho	3.3%	0.3%	1.0%	0.0%	0.0%	95.0%	0.3%	300
Illinois	1.3%	0.5%	0.8%	0.0%	0.1%	96.9%	0.4%	4,128
Indiana	2.5%	0.6%	0.8%	0.0%	0.0%	95.4%	0.8%	1,296
Iowa	3.0%	0.3%	0.8%	0.0%	0.0%	95.6%	0.3%	366
Kansas	2.9%	0.4%	1.1%	0.0%	0.0%	95.7%	0.0%	277
Kentucky	3.4%	0.7%	0.9%	0.0%	0.0%	94.8%	0.2%	536
Louisiana	2.6%	0.3%	0.6%	0.0%	0.0%	96.2%	0.3%	718
Maine	2.8%	0.4%	0.8%	0.0%	0.0%	94.8%	1.2%	250
Maryland	3.4%	0.7%	1.0%	0.0%	0.4%	93.7%	0.7%	2,583
Massachusetts	3.0%	0.6%	0.7%	0.0%	0.1%	94.7%	0.9%	1,443
Michigan	2.1%	0.5%	0.5%	0.1%	0.2%	95.9%	0.8%	1,671
Minnesota	1.6%	0.6%	0.2%	0.0%	0.3%	97.3%	0.0%	1,093
Mississippi	3.6%	0.5%	0.5%	0.0%	0.0%	94.3%	1.0%	385
Missouri	2.6%	0.9%	0.4%	0.0%	0.1%	95.9%	0.2%	1,051
Montana	3.7%	0.9%	0.0%	0.0%	0.0%	94.4%	0.9%	107
Nebraska	3.0%	0.0%	0.0%	0.0%	0.0%	96.4%	0.5%	197
Nevada	1.9%	0.8%	0.8%	0.1%	0.1%	95.8%	0.5%	1,131
New Hampshire	2.8%	0.0%	0.4%	0.0%	0.0%	94.7%	2.1%	284
New Jersey	1.6%	0.5%	0.7%	0.0%	0.1%	96.4%	0.7%	3,482
New Mexico	1.6%	0.3%	0.3%	0.0%	0.3%	97.1%	0.5%	381
New York	1.5%	0.6%	0.5%	0.0%	0.3%	94.3%	2.7%	4,313
North Carolina	2.9%	0.4%	0.9%	0.0%	0.1%	95.3%	0.4%	2,459
North Dakota	0.0%	0.0%	0.0%	0.0%	0.0%	100.0%	0.0%	26
Ohio	2.3%	0.5%	0.2%	0.0%	0.0%	96.5%	0.5%	2,169
Oklahoma	1.6%	1.1%	0.0%	0.0%	0.0%	97.3%	0.0%	377
Oregon	1.9%	0.5%	0.1%	0.0%	0.4%	96.1%	0.9%	775
Pennsylvania	2.4%	0.4%	0.7%	0.0%	0.0%	95.5%	1.0%	2,562
Rhode Island	3.1%	0.3%	1.0%	0.0%	0.0%	94.8%	0.7%	291
South Carolina	4.1%	0.8%	0.5%	0.0%	0.0%	94.2%	0.4%	1,066
South Dakota	4.1%	0.0%	0.0%	0.0%	0.0%	95.9%	0.0%	49
Tennessee	2.9%	0.5%	0.7%	0.0%	0.1%	95.5%	0.3%	1,003
Texas	3.1%	1.0%	0.7%	0.0%	0.1%	94.7%	0.4%	3,775
Utah	3.5%	0.0%	0.4%	0.0%	0.0%	95.5%	0.6%	510
Vermont	1.8%	0.9%	0.0%	0.0%	0.0%	97.2%	0.0%	109
Virginia	3.1%	0.8%	0.8%	0.0%	0.2%	94.1%	0.9%	1,709
Washington	2.1%	0.7%	0.9%	0.0%	0.3%	95.4%	0.6%	1,698
West Virginia	6.3%	1.1%	1.1%	0.0%	0.0%	90.3%	1.1%	175
Wisconsin	2.2%	0.5%	0.5%	0.0%	0.0%	96.9%	0.0%	880
Wyoming	2.1%	0.0%	0.0%	0.0%	0.0%	97.9%	0.0%	48
Other	0.7%	0.0%	0.0%	0.0%	0.0%	99.3%	0.0%	136

Table 57. Number of Modification Actions in Combination Actions Implemented in the Fourth Quarter of 2013						
States	Capitalization	Rate Reduction or Freeze	Term Extension	Principal Reduction	Principal Deferral	Total Combination Modifications
Total - All States	61,402	59,592	54,592	7,625	22,065	69,096
Alabama	734	729	698	36	172	832
Alaska	41	33	38	2	5	43
Arizona	991	980	894	153	431	1,161
Arkansas	280	302	287	13	82	336
California	9,085	8,051	6,348	2,334	3,369	9,691
Colorado	669	707	637	39	139	807
Connecticut	1,002	945	848	129	336	1,103
Delaware	361	345	343	18	121	405
District of Columbia	124	101	98	18	37	132
Florida	7,110	6,464	5,870	1,252	3,252	7,660
Georgia	2,598	2,701	2,482	233	1,117	3,042
Hawaii	153	133	115	13	38	156
Idaho	241	255	239	12	70	285
Illinois	3,526	3,441	3,319	446	1,694	3,999
Indiana	1,014	1,107	1,078	58	314	1,236
Iowa	294	311	307	8	51	350
Kansas	220	224	226	6	50	265
Kentucky	458	453	421	12	110	508
Louisiana	618	614	550	29	128	691
Maine	216	202	192	16	55	237
Maryland	2,104	2,033	1,849	300	868	2,421
Massachusetts	1,240	1,142	1,112	136	400	1,366
Michigan	1,442	1,393	1,296	144	541	1,602
Minnesota	906	925	909	58	283	1,063
Mississippi	325	328	278	25	70	363
Missouri	848	908	812	79	259	1,008
Montana	88	89	83	3	20	101
Nebraska	156	164	166	4	27	190
Nevada	959	878	797	199	497	1,083
New Hampshire	243	235	209	30	75	269
New Jersey	3,030	2,856	2,806	333	1,139	3,356
New Mexico	321	332	313	29	100	370
New York	3,798	3,469	3,287	300	1,294	4,069
North Carolina	2,038	2,053	1,924	135	564	2,343
North Dakota	24	23	25	0	7	26
Ohio	1,738	1,902	1,808	116	544	2,093
Oklahoma	320	316	312	12	73	367
Oregon	677	637	619	54	198	745
Pennsylvania	2,125	2,122	2,059	147	652	2,447
Rhode Island	243	225	204	47	104	276
South Carolina	893	898	819	61	280	1,004
South Dakota	44	40	37	6	7	47
Tennessee	826	868	740	70	220	958
Texas	2,878	3,293	3,063	121	1,022	3,575
Utah	401	433	402	39	102	487
Vermont	101	90	86	3	20	106
Virginia	1,378	1,401	1,276	127	389	1,609
Washington	1,433	1,398	1,340	139	451	1,620
West Virginia	145	133	125	10	33	158
Wisconsin	770	741	700	61	234	853
Wyoming	41	46	35	3	11	47
Other	132	123	111	7	10	135

Table 58. Percentage of Modification Actions in Combination Actions Implemented in the Fourth Quarter of 2013					
States	Capitalization	Rate Reduction or Freeze	Term Extension	Principal Reduction	Principal Deferral	Total Combination Modifications
Total - All States	88.9%	86.2%	79.0%	11.0%	31.9%	69,096
Alabama	88.2%	87.6%	83.9%	4.3%	20.7%	832
Alaska	95.3%	76.7%	88.4%	4.7%	11.6%	43
Arizona	85.4%	84.4%	77.0%	13.2%	37.1%	1,161
Arkansas	83.3%	89.9%	85.4%	3.9%	24.4%	336
California	93.7%	83.1%	65.5%	24.1%	34.8%	9,691
Colorado	82.9%	87.6%	78.9%	4.8%	17.2%	807
Connecticut	90.8%	85.7%	76.9%	11.7%	30.5%	1,103
Delaware	89.1%	85.2%	84.7%	4.4%	29.9%	405
District of Columbia	93.9%	76.5%	74.2%	13.6%	28.0%	132
Florida	92.8%	84.4%	76.6%	16.3%	42.5%	7,660
Georgia	85.4%	88.8%	81.6%	7.7%	36.7%	3,042
Hawaii	98.1%	85.3%	73.7%	8.3%	24.4%	156
Idaho	84.6%	89.5%	83.9%	4.2%	24.6%	285
Illinois	88.2%	86.0%	83.0%	11.2%	42.4%	3,999
Indiana	82.0%	89.6%	87.2%	4.7%	25.4%	1,236
Iowa	84.0%	88.9%	87.7%	2.3%	14.6%	350
Kansas	83.0%	84.5%	85.3%	2.3%	18.9%	265
Kentucky	90.2%	89.2%	82.9%	2.4%	21.7%	508
Louisiana	89.4%	88.9%	79.6%	4.2%	18.5%	691
Maine	91.1%	85.2%	81.0%	6.8%	23.2%	237
Maryland	86.9%	84.0%	76.4%	12.4%	35.9%	2,421
Massachusetts	90.8%	83.6%	81.4%	10.0%	29.3%	1,366
Michigan	90.0%	87.0%	80.9%	9.0%	33.8%	1,602
Minnesota	85.2%	87.0%	85.5%	5.5%	26.6%	1,063
Mississippi	89.5%	90.4%	76.6%	6.9%	19.3%	363
Missouri	84.1%	90.1%	80.6%	7.8%	25.7%	1,008
Montana	87.1%	88.1%	82.2%	3.0%	19.8%	101
Nebraska	82.1%	86.3%	87.4%	2.1%	14.2%	190
Nevada	88.6%	81.1%	73.6%	18.4%	45.9%	1,083
New Hampshire	90.3%	87.4%	77.7%	11.2%	27.9%	269
New Jersey	90.3%	85.1%	83.6%	9.9%	33.9%	3,356
New Mexico	86.8%	89.7%	84.6%	7.8%	27.0%	370
New York	93.3%	85.3%	80.8%	7.4%	31.8%	4,069
North Carolina	87.0%	87.6%	82.1%	5.8%	24.1%	2,343
North Dakota	92.3%	88.5%	96.2%	0.0%	26.9%	26
Ohio	83.0%	90.9%	86.4%	5.5%	26.0%	2,093
Oklahoma	87.2%	86.1%	85.0%	3.3%	19.9%	367
Oregon	90.9%	85.5%	83.1%	7.2%	26.6%	745
Pennsylvania	86.8%	86.7%	84.1%	6.0%	26.6%	2,447
Rhode Island	88.0%	81.5%	73.9%	17.0%	37.7%	276
South Carolina	88.9%	89.4%	81.6%	6.1%	27.9%	1,004
South Dakota	93.6%	85.1%	78.7%	12.8%	14.9%	47
Tennessee	86.2%	90.6%	77.2%	7.3%	23.0%	958
Texas	80.5%	92.1%	85.7%	3.4%	28.6%	3,575
Utah	82.3%	88.9%	82.5%	8.0%	20.9%	487
Vermont	95.3%	84.9%	81.1%	2.8%	18.9%	106
Virginia	85.6%	87.1%	79.3%	7.9%	24.2%	1,609
Washington	88.5%	86.3%	82.7%	8.6%	27.8%	1,620
West Virginia	91.8%	84.2%	79.1%	6.3%	20.9%	158
Wisconsin	90.3%	86.9%	82.1%	7.2%	27.4%	853
Wyoming	87.2%	97.9%	74.5%	6.4%	23.4%	47
Other	97.8%	91.1%	82.2%	5.2%	7.4%	135

States	Decreased by 20% or More	Decreased by 10% to Less Than 20%	Decreased by Less Than 10%	Unchanged	Increased	Not Reported	Total Modifications
Total - All States	46,511	12,154	6,872	933	5,550	446	72,466
Alabama	519	158	91	18	78	1	865
Alaska	22	10	6	0	5	0	43
Arizona	781	221	105	20	88	4	1,219
Arkansas	211	64	34	6	33	1	349
California	6,623	1,562	1,018	141	854	66	10,264
Colorado	492	182	93	21	71	4	863
Connecticut	770	180	121	12	72	9	1,164
Delaware	250	87	47	7	21	0	412
District of Columbia	74	28	27	2	17	1	149
Florida	5,435	1,087	700	63	632	48	7,965
Georgia	2,143	502	272	53	205	19	3,194
Hawaii	109	20	27	2	12	0	170
Idaho	185	54	30	4	25	2	300
Illinois	2,942	587	311	37	236	15	4,128
Indiana	786	238	143	20	101	8	1,296
Iowa	216	81	32	5	32	0	366
Kansas	162	55	28	1	31	0	277
Kentucky	302	99	63	12	59	1	536
Louisiana	401	141	80	10	85	1	718
Maine	154	36	35	3	21	1	250
Maryland	1,560	468	273	39	222	21	2,583
Massachusetts	916	270	142	12	96	7	1,443
Michigan	1,167	247	125	22	101	9	1,671
Minnesota	710	211	92	16	58	6	1,093
Mississippi	221	57	49	3	51	4	385
Missouri	686	206	76	9	71	3	1,051
Montana	59	20	12	5	11	0	107
Nebraska	106	50	21	0	19	1	197
Nevada	809	152	86	17	57	10	1,131
New Hampshire	185	42	25	1	25	6	284
New Jersey	2,319	578	309	27	221	28	3,482
New Mexico	252	71	33	7	18	0	381
New York	2,836	687	369	45	290	86	4,313
North Carolina	1,476	456	268	39	211	9	2,459
North Dakota	12	3	7	1	3	0	26
Ohio	1,440	366	183	34	138	8	2,169
Oklahoma	210	73	39	6	49	0	377
Oregon	480	166	62	8	56	3	775
Pennsylvania	1,631	458	238	29	188	18	2,562
Rhode Island	191	49	29	3	17	2	291
South Carolina	631	199	115	11	105	5	1,066
South Dakota	26	10	8	0	5	0	49
Tennessee	621	191	88	16	84	3	1,003
Texas	2,252	724	394	64	325	16	3,775
Utah	298	113	41	8	48	2	510
Vermont	64	21	17	1	6	0	109
Virginia	948	330	221	31	172	7	1,709
Washington	1,025	321	183	19	142	8	1,698
West Virginia	103	26	15	8	21	2	175
Wisconsin	573	160	79	13	54	1	880
Wyoming	27	14	3	0	4	0	48
Other	100	23	7	2	4	0	136

Table 59. Changes in Monthly Principal and Interest Payments by State (Number)
Modifications Implemented in the Fourth Quarter of 2013

| Table 60. Changes in Monthly Principal and Interest Payments (Percentage) Modifications Implemented in the Fourth Quarter of 2013 | | | | | | |
States	Decreased by 20% or More	Decreased by 10% to Less Than 20%	Decreased by Less Than 10%	Unchanged	Increased	Not Reported	Total Modifications
Total - All States	64.2%	16.8%	9.5%	1.3%	7.7%	0.6%	72,466
Alabama	60.0%	18.3%	10.5%	2.1%	9.0%	0.1%	865
Alaska	51.2%	23.3%	14.0%	0.0%	11.6%	0.0%	43
Arizona	64.1%	18.1%	8.6%	1.6%	7.2%	0.3%	1,219
Arkansas	60.5%	18.3%	9.7%	1.7%	9.5%	0.3%	349
California	64.5%	15.2%	9.9%	1.4%	8.3%	0.6%	10,264
Colorado	57.0%	21.1%	10.8%	2.4%	8.2%	0.5%	863
Connecticut	66.2%	15.5%	10.4%	1.0%	6.2%	0.8%	1,164
Delaware	60.7%	21.1%	11.4%	1.7%	5.1%	0.0%	412
District of Columbia	49.7%	18.8%	18.1%	1.3%	11.4%	0.7%	149
Florida	68.2%	13.6%	8.8%	0.8%	7.9%	0.6%	7,965
Georgia	67.1%	15.7%	8.5%	1.7%	6.4%	0.6%	3,194
Hawaii	64.1%	11.8%	15.9%	1.2%	7.1%	0.0%	170
Idaho	61.7%	18.0%	10.0%	1.3%	8.3%	0.7%	300
Illinois	71.3%	14.2%	7.5%	0.9%	5.7%	0.4%	4,128
Indiana	60.6%	18.4%	11.0%	1.5%	7.8%	0.6%	1,296
Iowa	59.0%	22.1%	8.7%	1.4%	8.7%	0.0%	366
Kansas	58.5%	19.9%	10.1%	0.4%	11.2%	0.0%	277
Kentucky	56.3%	18.5%	11.8%	2.2%	11.0%	0.2%	536
Louisiana	55.8%	19.6%	11.1%	1.4%	11.8%	0.1%	718
Maine	61.6%	14.4%	14.0%	1.2%	8.4%	0.4%	250
Maryland	60.4%	18.1%	10.6%	1.5%	8.6%	0.8%	2,583
Massachusetts	63.5%	18.7%	9.8%	0.8%	6.7%	0.5%	1,443
Michigan	69.8%	14.8%	7.5%	1.3%	6.0%	0.5%	1,671
Minnesota	65.0%	19.3%	8.4%	1.5%	5.3%	0.5%	1,093
Mississippi	57.4%	14.8%	12.7%	0.8%	13.2%	1.0%	385
Missouri	65.3%	19.6%	7.2%	0.9%	6.8%	0.3%	1,051
Montana	55.1%	18.7%	11.2%	4.7%	10.3%	0.0%	107
Nebraska	53.8%	25.4%	10.7%	0.0%	9.6%	0.5%	197
Nevada	71.5%	13.4%	7.6%	1.5%	5.0%	0.9%	1,131
New Hampshire	65.1%	14.8%	8.8%	0.4%	8.8%	2.1%	284
New Jersey	66.6%	16.6%	8.9%	0.8%	6.3%	0.8%	3,482
New Mexico	66.1%	18.6%	8.7%	1.8%	4.7%	0.0%	381
New York	65.8%	15.9%	8.6%	1.0%	6.7%	2.0%	4,313
North Carolina	60.0%	18.5%	10.9%	1.6%	8.6%	0.4%	2,459
North Dakota	46.2%	11.5%	26.9%	3.8%	11.5%	0.0%	26
Ohio	66.4%	16.9%	8.4%	1.6%	6.4%	0.4%	2,169
Oklahoma	55.7%	19.4%	10.3%	1.6%	13.0%	0.0%	377
Oregon	61.9%	21.4%	8.0%	1.0%	7.2%	0.4%	775
Pennsylvania	63.7%	17.9%	9.3%	1.1%	7.3%	0.7%	2,562
Rhode Island	65.6%	16.8%	10.0%	1.0%	5.8%	0.7%	291
South Carolina	59.2%	18.7%	10.8%	1.0%	9.8%	0.5%	1,066
South Dakota	53.1%	20.4%	16.3%	0.0%	10.2%	0.0%	49
Tennessee	61.9%	19.0%	8.8%	1.6%	8.4%	0.3%	1,003
Texas	59.7%	19.2%	10.4%	1.7%	8.6%	0.4%	3,775
Utah	58.4%	22.2%	8.0%	1.6%	9.4%	0.4%	510
Vermont	58.7%	19.3%	15.6%	0.9%	5.5%	0.0%	109
Virginia	55.5%	19.3%	12.9%	1.8%	10.1%	0.4%	1,709
Washington	60.4%	18.9%	10.8%	1.1%	8.4%	0.5%	1,698
West Virginia	58.9%	14.9%	8.6%	4.6%	12.0%	1.1%	175
Wisconsin	65.1%	18.2%	9.0%	1.5%	6.1%	0.1%	880
Wyoming	56.3%	29.2%	6.3%	0.0%	8.3%	0.0%	48
Other	73.5%	16.9%	5.1%	1.5%	2.9%	0.0%	136

Table 61. Number of Re-Defaults for Loans Modified in the Second Quarter of 2013
(60 or More Days Delinquent After 6 Months by Changes in Monthly Principal and Interest Payments)

States	Decreased by 20% or More	Decreased by 10% to Less Than 20%	Decreased by Less Than 10%	Unchanged	Increased	Not Reported	Total Modifications
Total - All States	5,121	3,300	2,860	158	1,574	41	13,054
Alabama	76	54	55	5	22	1	213
Alaska	2	2	2	0	1	0	7
Arizona	71	60	47	0	19	1	198
Arkansas	34	31	25	1	15	0	106
California	484	216	188	19	144	9	1,060
Colorado	46	45	36	2	22	0	151
Connecticut	91	41	30	4	25	0	191
Delaware	22	22	13	1	10	0	68
District of Columbia	8	6	6	2	3	0	25
Florida	466	205	187	15	119	1	993
Georgia	295	226	216	7	77	3	824
Hawaii	6	6	4	0	3	0	19
Idaho	12	12	13	0	8	0	45
Illinois	338	166	144	10	87	0	745
Indiana	113	75	92	2	46	2	330
Iowa	25	21	23	0	7	0	76
Kansas	35	22	19	2	12	2	92
Kentucky	43	46	28	2	19	1	139
Louisiana	74	54	63	1	27	0	219
Maine	15	13	7	1	3	0	39
Maryland	192	134	117	5	60	1	509
Massachusetts	118	74	53	6	33	2	286
Michigan	136	84	64	3	35	0	322
Minnesota	78	51	20	1	27	0	177
Mississippi	46	17	25	1	10	1	100
Missouri	98	62	40	2	41	0	243
Montana	9	4	7	0	1	0	21
Nebraska	19	14	11	3	4	0	51
Nevada	55	36	21	3	11	0	126
New Hampshire	22	11	13	0	5	0	51
New Jersey	233	125	116	5	56	2	537
New Mexico	26	24	8	2	5	1	66
New York	288	153	111	3	76	2	633
North Carolina	179	157	138	11	65	3	553
North Dakota	0	0	1	0	2	0	3
Ohio	201	106	112	5	69	0	493
Oklahoma	47	32	29	0	14	0	122
Oregon	48	25	13	0	10	0	96
Pennsylvania	216	123	101	2	81	3	526
Rhode Island	23	13	10	0	7	0	53
South Carolina	81	65	64	3	30	1	244
South Dakota	1	6	2	0	2	0	11
Tennessee	114	66	57	5	27	0	269
Texas	334	330	288	9	125	2	1,088
Utah	26	31	31	1	9	0	98
Vermont	2	3	5	1	2	0	13
Virginia	104	94	82	5	40	1	326
Washington	88	65	69	2	28	2	254
West Virginia	13	16	10	0	4	0	43
Wisconsin	64	53	40	4	24	0	185
Wyoming	0	2	1	1	2	0	6
Other	4	1	3	1	0	0	9

States	Decreased by 20% or More	Decreased by 10% to Less Than 20%	Decreased by Less Than 10%	Unchanged	Increased	Not Reported	Total Modifications
Table 62. Re-Default Rates for Loans Modified in the Second Quarter of 2013 (Percentage) (60 or More Days Delinquent After 6 Months by Changes in Monthly Principal and Interest Payments)							
Total - All States	9.2%	15.8%	23.5%	18.1%	27.1%	15.5%	13.6%
Alabama	13.0%	19.2%	33.3%	71.4%	37.3%	25.0%	19.3%
Alaska	9.5%	18.2%	15.4%	0.0%	33.3%	0.0%	14.6%
Arizona	7.0%	13.8%	22.2%	0.0%	20.9%	14.3%	11.1%
Arkansas	16.4%	22.5%	32.1%	100.0%	46.9%	0.0%	23.2%
California	5.0%	8.1%	11.3%	8.3%	13.8%	17.0%	6.9%
Colorado	7.5%	13.3%	18.4%	20.0%	27.2%	0.0%	12.1%
Connecticut	10.9%	14.6%	19.9%	40.0%	27.5%	0.0%	13.9%
Delaware	10.0%	18.8%	21.0%	20.0%	47.6%	0.0%	16.0%
District of Columbia	8.7%	11.8%	16.7%	100.0%	23.1%	0.0%	12.9%
Florida	7.0%	11.8%	17.7%	16.5%	20.6%	4.8%	9.8%
Georgia	10.3%	18.2%	31.2%	20.0%	29.4%	17.6%	16.2%
Hawaii	4.9%	13.3%	13.8%	0.0%	20.0%	0.0%	8.9%
Idaho	5.9%	14.1%	27.7%	0.0%	32.0%	0.0%	12.3%
Illinois	9.8%	16.8%	25.5%	25.6%	34.3%	0.0%	14.1%
Indiana	13.9%	20.1%	33.1%	25.0%	32.9%	100.0%	20.4%
Iowa	11.4%	15.9%	30.7%	0.0%	20.0%	0.0%	16.3%
Kansas	13.1%	17.1%	27.1%	28.6%	46.2%	40.0%	18.2%
Kentucky	12.5%	26.4%	26.7%	25.0%	38.0%	100.0%	20.4%
Louisiana	14.4%	23.3%	37.5%	10.0%	31.8%	0.0%	21.6%
Maine	10.9%	17.1%	17.9%	50.0%	13.0%	0.0%	14.1%
Maryland	10.8%	16.3%	24.4%	17.9%	33.0%	11.1%	15.5%
Massachusetts	10.4%	18.4%	24.4%	40.0%	34.0%	20.0%	15.3%
Michigan	10.2%	16.5%	26.1%	33.3%	31.3%	0.0%	14.6%
Minnesota	10.7%	19.2%	12.3%	11.1%	30.0%	0.0%	14.1%
Mississippi	14.6%	15.3%	29.1%	14.3%	30.3%	100.0%	18.1%
Missouri	12.7%	18.1%	23.7%	20.0%	42.7%	0.0%	17.5%
Montana	13.2%	13.3%	29.2%	0.0%	33.3%	0.0%	16.5%
Nebraska	13.7%	23.7%	31.4%	75.0%	30.8%	0.0%	20.3%
Nevada	6.2%	14.2%	16.8%	23.1%	18.6%	0.0%	9.3%
New Hampshire	11.1%	15.5%	35.1%	0.0%	22.7%	0.0%	15.5%
New Jersey	10.1%	16.3%	27.2%	14.3%	30.4%	18.2%	14.4%
New Mexico	11.1%	18.5%	11.8%	33.3%	19.2%	50.0%	14.2%
New York	8.6%	14.7%	18.6%	11.1%	29.8%	18.2%	12.0%
North Carolina	11.6%	19.6%	30.1%	29.7%	32.7%	27.3%	18.1%
North Dakota	0.0%	0.0%	25.0%	0.0%	40.0%	0.0%	11.5%
Ohio	12.5%	16.2%	26.8%	21.7%	35.6%	0.0%	17.0%
Oklahoma	15.7%	17.2%	28.2%	0.0%	33.3%	0.0%	19.3%
Oregon	8.0%	10.5%	10.1%	0.0%	19.6%	0.0%	9.3%
Pennsylvania	13.0%	20.7%	27.3%	7.4%	35.8%	21.4%	18.2%
Rhode Island	10.8%	17.6%	22.7%	0.0%	58.3%	0.0%	15.5%
South Carolina	11.2%	18.8%	29.6%	33.3%	29.1%	33.3%	17.4%
South Dakota	4.0%	30.0%	25.0%	0.0%	25.0%	0.0%	17.7%
Tennessee	15.3%	19.4%	26.3%	33.3%	32.1%	0.0%	19.2%
Texas	12.9%	20.2%	35.2%	30.0%	36.1%	16.7%	20.0%
Utah	6.8%	15.7%	22.3%	20.0%	25.0%	0.0%	12.8%
Vermont	4.0%	13.6%	38.5%	100.0%	28.6%	0.0%	14.0%
Virginia	8.6%	14.5%	23.0%	18.5%	26.1%	16.7%	13.6%
Washington	6.9%	13.5%	22.1%	11.1%	19.2%	28.6%	11.4%
West Virginia	12.6%	34.0%	28.6%	0.0%	18.2%	0.0%	19.9%
Wisconsin	10.5%	20.0%	25.8%	40.0%	31.6%	0.0%	16.6%
Wyoming	0.0%	14.3%	11.1%	100.0%	33.3%	0.0%	12.2%
Other	3.8%	5.0%	23.1%	100.0%	0.0%	0.0%	6.2%

Index of Tables

Table 1. Number of New Home Retention Actions..5

Table 2. Status of Mortgages Modified in 2008–3Q 2013 6

Table 3. Re-Default Rates for Portfolio Loans and Loans Serviced for Others 7

Table 4. New Foreclosures and Foreclosures in Process 7

Table 5. Completed Foreclosures and Other Home Forfeiture Actions 7

Table 6. Overall Mortgage Portfolio..11

Table 7. Overall Portfolio Performance...12

Table 8. Performance of Mortgages Held by Reporting Banks and Thrift (Percentage)* 13

Table 9. Performance of Government-Guaranteed Mortgages (Percentage)..........................14

Table 10. Performance of GSE Mortgages (Percentage)..15

Table 11. Seriously Delinquent Mortgages, by Risk Category 16

Table 12. Mortgages 30 to 59 Days Delinquent, by Risk Category 17

Table 13. Number of New Home Retention Actions..18

Table 14. HAMP Modifications, by Investor and Risk Category...19

Table 15. HAMP Trial-Period Plans, by Investor and Risk Category.....................................19

Table 16. Percentage of New Home Retention Actions Relative to Newly Initiated Foreclosures, by Risk Category..20

Table 17. Changes in Loan Terms for Modifications Through the Fourth Quarter of 2013 21

Table 18. Changes in Loan Terms for HAMP Modifications Through the Fourth Quarter of 2013 22

Table 19. Changes in Loan Terms for Modifications, by Risk Category, During the Fourth Quarter of 2013 23

Table 20. Type of Modification Action, by Investor and Product Type, During the Fourth Quarter of 2013 24

Table 21. Type of HAMP Modification Action, by Investor and Product Type, During the Fourth Quarter of 2013 25

Table 22. Changes in Monthly Principal and Interest Payments Resulting From Modifications 27

Table 23. Changes in Monthly Principal and Interest Payments Resulting From HAMP Modifications 28

Table 24. Average Change in Monthly Payments Resulting From Modifications, by Quarter* 29

Table 25. Modified Loans 60 or More Days Delinquent..30

Table 26. Modified Loans 30 or More Days Delinquent.. 31

Table 27. Modified Loans 90 or More Days Delinquent*.. 32

Table 28. Re-Default Rates for Portfolio Loans and Loans Serviced
for Others Modified in 2008 33

Table 29. Re-Default Rates for Portfolio Loans and Loans Serviced
for Others Modified in 2009 33

Table 30. Re-Default Rates for Portfolio Loans and Loans Serviced
for Others Modified in 2010 33

Table 31. Re-Default Rates for Portfolio Loans and Loans Serviced
for Others Modified in 2011 34

Table 32. Re-Default Rates for Portfolio Loans and Loans Serviced
for Others Modified in 2012 34

Table 33. Re-Default Rates for Portfolio Loans and Loans Serviced
for Others Modified in 2013 34

Table 34. Performance of HAMP Modifications Compared With Other Modifications 35

Table 35. Re-Default Rates of Loans Modified in 2008 by Change in Payment 36

Table 36. Re-Default Rates of Loans Modified in 2009 by Change in Payment 36

Table 37. Re-Default Rates of Loans Modified in 2010 by Change in Payment 37

Table 38. Re-Default Rates of Loans Modified in 2011 by Change in Payment 37

Table 39. Re-Default Rates of Loans Modified in 2012 by Change in Payment 37

Table 40. Re-Default Rates of Loans Modified in 2013 by Change in Payment 37

Table 41. 60+ Delinquency at Six Months After Modification by Change
in Monthly Payment.. 38

Table 42. Status of Mortgages Modified in 2008–3Q 2013 39

Table 43. Completed Foreclosures and Other Home Forfeiture Actions 40

Table 44. Number of Newly Initiated Foreclosures.. 41

Table 45. Foreclosures in Process... 42

Table 46. Completed Foreclosures 43

Table 47. Completed Short Sales and Deeds in Lieu of Foreclosure 44

Table 48. Percentage of New Home Retention Actions Relative to Forfeiture Actions,
by Risk Category... 45

Table 49. Number of New Loan Modifications... 46

Table 50. Number of New Trial-Period Plans 47

Table 51. Number of New Payment Plans 48

Table 52. Changes in Terms for Modifications Made Through the Fourth Quarter of 2013 49

Table 53. Changes in Terms for Combination Modifications Through
the Fourth Quarter of 2013 50

Table 54. Number and Percentage of Mortgage Modifications 52

Table 55. Number of Mortgage Modification Actions 53

Table 56. Percentage of Mortgage Modification Actions 54

Table 57. Number of Modification Actions in Combination Actions 55

Table 58. Percentage of Modification Actions in Combination Actions 56

Table 59. Changes in Monthly Principal and Interest Payments by State (Number) 57

Table 60. Changes in Monthly Principal and Interest Payments (Percentage) 58

Table 61. Number of Re-Defaults for Loans Modified in the Second Quarter of 2013 59

Table 62. Re-Default Rates for Loans Modified in the Second Quarter of 2013 (Percentage) ... 60

Index of Figures

Figure 1. Portfolio Composition.. 11

Figure 2. Overall Portfolio Performance 12

Figure 3. Performance of Mortgages Held by Reporting Banks and Thrift................ 13

Figure 4. Performance of Government-Guaranteed Mortgages 14

Figure 5. Performance of GSE Mortgages 15

Figure 6. Seriously Delinquent Mortgages, by Risk Category................................... 16

Figure 7. Mortgages 30 to 59 Days Delinquent, by Risk Category 17

Figure 8. Number of New Home Retention Actions.. 18

Figure 9. New Home Retention Actions Relative to Newly Initiated Foreclosures,
by Risk Category.. 20

Figure 10. Changes in Monthly Principal and Interest Payments 27

Figure 11. Modified Loans 60 or More Days Delinquent... 30

Figure 12. Modified Loans 30 or More Days Delinquent... 31

Figure 13. Modified Loans 90 or More Days Delinquent... 32

Figure 14. 60+ Delinquency at Six Months After Modification by Change
in Monthly Payment... 38

Figure 15. Number of Newly Initiated Foreclosures.. 41

Figure 16. Number of Foreclosures in Process 42

Figure 17. Number of Completed Foreclosures 43

Figure 18. Number of Completed Short Sales and Deeds in Lieu of Foreclosure 44

Figure 19. Percentage of New Home Retention Actions Relative to Forfeiture Actions,
by Risk Category.. 45

Figure 20. Number of New Loan Modifications... 46

Figure 21. Number of New Trial-Period Plans 47

Figure 22. Number of New Payment Plans 48

www.ingramcontent.com/pod-product-compliance
Lightning Source LLC
Chambersburg PA
CBHW080537290526
45790CB00006B/2448